A vivid look at life as [obscured] stories that will have you [obscured] challenging look at how we [obscured] really be living for Jesus.

Laura Wilkinson,
Olympic & World Champion Diver

♦

Get ready to make a new friend. Carrie Anne Hudson's *Redefining Home* is that rich conversation over coffee you've longed for in a book. Her thoughts & experiences nourish the heart with a good laugh, a needed cry, a clearer view, a new perspective and a deeper devotion.

Donna Stuart,
Wife to Breakaway Ministries Director,
Ben Stuart; Songwriter/Worship Leader

♦

Honesty creates a context for freedom, defeats shame, removes us from isolation and reminds us that we are human. Carrie Anne Hudson in *Redefining Home* has been masterfully honest with her life transplanted across the water. She causes you to think, laugh, hurt and pray by taking courage in her story, family, and global urgency. Honest stories empower, touch, engage, and move you to action. Her and her family's life on display is a discipleship tool for those loving others in missional community.

Jerrell Altic,
Pastor of Mobilization, Houston's FBC

I LOVED *Redefining Home*! There were so many beautiful moments where I was laughing hysterically. Carrie paints pictures of daily life in China that are acutely aware of the juxtaposition of culture existing in a foreign country while noticing the nuances of beauty that surround her life. As a mother of three I loved getting to see life through her eyes.

Jamie Wells,
Artist; Co-founder
www.ImagoDei.pro and www.Artworship.org

◆

I love reading Carrie's story because I find so much of our family in theirs. Life overseas is a melting pot of confusion, humor, difficulty, and trust in God that is often difficult to describe, and yet she packages it in such an effortless way. If there is one family on earth I could choose to be a fly on the wall with, it just might possibly be the Hudson's. Read this book! It's like my dream come true.

Joy Parker, Worker in Thailand

# Redefining HOME

*Squatty Potties, Split Pants,
and Other Things that
Divide My World*

# Redefining HOME

## Squatty Potties, Split Pants, and Other Things that Divide My World

CARRIE ANNE HUDSON

LUCIDBOOKS

# Seasons of Our Life

To Jackson and the kids.
For your genuine laughter and hopeful joy.

# Who We Are

"'You come of the Lord Adam and the Lady Eve,' said Aslan.
'And that is both honor enough to erect the head of the
poorest beggar, and shame enough to bow the
shoulders of the greatest emperor in earth.'"

*Prince Caspian* by C.S. Lewis

*foreign everything*

**WE are the foreigners.**

I was carried 8,000 miles from the perfectly manicured bricks and highways that constructed my childhood to land in a culture that eats pickled cabbage for breakfast and refers to me as a long nosed foreigner. The miles separating the two would only begin to define the distance that I would travel be traveled as my paradigms shifted. China is a place defined by paradox. My western systems firmly in place, I began my life here with one child and lofty notions of my eventual popularity and impact. I soon realized that while people wanted pictures of me and a quick chat about the NBA, I was still an odd entity.

As I dodged sulking donkeys, waddling babies, boxes of soymilk, and screaming egg vendors, I became deafened by the loud droves of people rushing to nowhere. My ears picked up noises but my heart couldn't distinguish the sounds. I took in the garlicky air of a culture so opposite mine that we even pee and count money differently. It was as if someone had taken the colors, numbers and emotions that I had always known as constant and stuck them in a box. Then they took that box, shook it up, threw it down the stairs, peeled apart the sides, and dumped the contents out on a table. I couldn't make sense of a single thing as I tried to set up a home in this new place.

As I became slightly more proficient in the language, I began to understand. I saw the pushy grandmother at the market as a mere product of coming into adulthood during a time when food was a luxury and freedom was prohibited to enter any dreams-even at night. My American mantras of self-sufficiency and diligent individualism began to melt into reminders that my time was not my own and I was to see others as Jesus saw them.

As a Christian, I am personally reflecting what it means to be "aliens and strangers in the world," in light of being a foreigner in another country.

## *before we start*

Before we get started I have a few disclaimers. First of all, not all places in China are the same. Everything is true somewhere. To lump 1.4 billion people into a category is messy. Just as we wouldn't expect a socialite in Manhattan to even speak the same language as a farmer from Idaho, different places require different categories. This is our family's experience living as individualistic Americans in collectivist China. And even in this small slice of experience it is chaotic at times. We often joke that living here can be summarized in the phrase "Nothing is as it seems." Secondly, for various reasons I have changed most of the names in the book. But for better or for worse, all the events are still true.

In China, there are very strict rules that very few follow; there are millions of dollars being spent to make the world's fastest train system, but very little being spent putting trashcans on the streets; people hover over their children to make sure they never scrape a knee, yet put a plastic ring around a newborn's neck to let it float in a pool. We have told ourselves that asking the question 'why' is a dangerous one. We have learned to accept things as they are dealt to us and try hard not to get smacked upside the head in the process.

As I write, my family and I will play the role of "foreigner." I use this word to describe our life here because when we walk around the streets, our ears have grown accustomed to hearing the Chinese word for foreigner. It literally means "outside the country people." In our world, all things not ethnically Chinese are called foreign.

Most families in China have two parents, two grandparents, and one child all living under one roof. The two parents go out to work in the city while the grandmother stays at home, watches after the child, and makes noodles for dinner. The grandfather will head out early to his mahjong game tucked under a neighbor's magnolia tree. Our family moves in with an adult to child ratio that looks a little different with two parents and five kids. My rational and logical husband Jackson is not quite sure how we ended up on this life trajectory, but here we are.

I started writing because honestly, I realized that I had stopped laughing. The places that used to draw a smile…now only conjured deadpan indifference. I had let life strangle the curiosity out of my soul. So I went on a journey to recapture my humanity and in the process found hope and even a little laughter. There are times in the writing that I will be looking backwards, times I will be looking forwards, but no matter the day I will always remain looking.

Ok, here we go.

## decaf, 10 year plans and other pointless things

I graduated from Texas A&M back when using the Internet meant sending a typed message to the person's computer that sat immediately next to you. There was no Google or Facebook or becoming a licensed priest online. At that point, I had dreams of being this globetrotting, sassy, single girl who ate chapattis from sweaty street vendors in India and work in remote villages bringing medical care and hope to the hurting. I had no time for marriage, kids, or a job that required me to wear a dress. I would marry late and have kids even later. I certainly would never homeschool my children because clearly I was so talented that I didn't need to 'waste' my time at home. And besides, home-schooled kids were quirky and wore jumpers…everyday. Those same homeschooled kids made astronomy jokes that nobody understood but laughed out of pity at those poor unsocialized children. I would live in some swanky but not too suburban town, take mysterious pictures of coffee shops and wear lime green graphic tees. It was all about me. It was all about avoiding things that I didn't want to do.

Vain ambitions defined me as God was gently writing a future where I became a minor character. When I look back on who I used to be, I am embarrassed at the trivialities that caught my eye and fixed my gaze. My affections were shallow and misplaced.

Somewhere along the way, it became a trend to write down a ten-year plan. I'm pretty sure this exercise is recommended so that we can mock it all later on. A decade or so after scribbling a few things down, I looked at my life and there was not one thing happening that I had written on my 10-year plan. I got married at 22, started having babies at 25, moved to China, homeschooled all five of my children and took an exotic job working as a housewife. When people ask me how we got here, I shrug my shoulders and tell them I have no idea. But I do know that my eyes have been lifted off myself and onto the world that is wondrous in its expressions of the Creator.

And now I am writing. This is our journey as we visited the States, returned home to China and began searching for normal, yet again. I'm writing not because my world is so magnificent or extraordinary, but because life throws us things to look at and take in. So many times I am looking for shells in the shallow, when God is calling me to the treasures of the deep. While the depths are ominous and frightening, it is that very place that hides away color and beauty only seen by those willing to swim.

# American Culture Shock

"If you can speak three languages, you're trilingual.
If you can speak two languages, you're bilingual.
If you can speak only one language, you're an American."

Author Unknown

*When we landed in the States, we assumed that the transition would be fairly seamless. I mean Jackson and I both grew up here. What could possibly be different? Besides having to explain to my kids about such things as corn dogs, driveways, seat belts, and Velveeta cheese, we discovered that maybe we were outsiders in America too.*

### preparing is like hemorrhoid surgery

Preparing for such a big transition is like getting ready for hemorrhoid surgery. While you are excited about the result, the pain involved in getting there makes you cringe and sweat from every God given orifice you have.

The tickets had been bought and bags had been packed, yet my heart could never be prepared well enough for the few months we were about to spend in America. As we approached the States, I realized that I was afraid. Fitting back into American life was an impossibility. Our lives had changed too much to see things the same as before. I was scared that living in America would be like returning to your favorite pair of jeans only to realize that there was a huge hole in the crotch. You could never wear them comfortably again and you would certainly never wear them in public. At one time, those were your go-to jeans and now they are just a piece of fabric woven together by a history that doesn't resemble your future.

I wrote a few things down that my stomach wanted to vocalize as it kept me up at night with anxious fluttering and pangs. Since my stomach is bound up as a non-speaking organ, I decided to write them down for him. All of this happened each time I gave myself a picture of our life in the States for a few months:

I'm nervous that I won't have a clue what people are talking about. And when they mention things like who won American Idol or which teams made it to the Sweet 16, I will try to jump in with a story about eating duck blood soup and everyone will scatter like ants in the rain.

I'm nervous about going to church. That I will walk in the middle of a church building campaign meeting and want to scream ungodly things.

I'm nervous that my brain will forget every Chinese word I've ever learned.

I'm nervous that we will not have a place in our friend's lives.

I'm nervous that I won't be funny or interesting and will instead elicit blank stares and inner monologue mocking from others. They will then say things like, "Oh bless her heart, she lives in China."

I'm nervous that our kids will feel like outcasts.

I'm nervous that the comforts of America will make me lazy in my pursuit of Jesus.

I'm nervous that I will gain 83 pounds consuming cheese.

I'm nervous that I won't be able to hear God clearly because my ears will be log jammed with the familiar.

I'm nervous that the only reason people will want to have us over for dinner is because we live in China and people like to have friends who live internationally. Just like white people like to say they have a black friend.

## culture shock

Having moved back and forth from China to America several times, culture shock has become a familiar friend. I remember the first time we visited the States after living in China for almost a year. It was as if my eyes had been plucked out and I had been given a whole new pair. I saw things that I had missed before. When I looked out my window, colors were different and people were weird. As we reunited with our American friends we realized that we used the same words, but were speaking a totally different language.

The first time I walked into a grocery store I got lost in the 73 choices of white bread. I was overwhelmed. I ran to the produce section so that the smells and shapes were at least semi-recognizable to me. The patterns of dotted fruit flies connected my two worlds in disheveled yet familiar shapes. As I shopped, I looked smugly into other people's carts and watched them purchase a $10 bottle of organic carrot juice. I immediately started calculating how many bowls of noodles that could buy for my friends in China.

It was 14.

I walked through the air-conditioned aisles in awe of how clean and organized things looked. Then I would try and find my yogurt girl who was able to tell me exactly where to go to find strawberry yogurt at home in China. She wasn't there. There is very little staff wandering about in American grocery stores. Probably because Americans don't want to be bothered with whatever other people want to suggest they should buy. There was corn-fed beef, brown cage-free eggs, turkey bacon, and sugar-free instant pudding in 17 different flavors. I felt like Alice in Wonderland as she tumbled down the long corridor following after the white rabbit. As I spun down, all the dairy, meat, bottles and bags went swirling around my head making me dizzy and disoriented. Choices. There were so many choices. And yet as I looked around, people looked annoyed at not being able to find exactly what they needed. Maybe what they needed wasn't going to be found in a purchase.

In my experience, people have one of two reactions upon returning to their home culture after living overseas. They either love being in America: rejoicing in driving a car, eating frozen dinners, and glancing at the sky every two minutes to comment on how incredibly blue it is. Or they get judgmental, depressed and skip the 4th of July parade because it's all just too much. I find that I oscillate between both of those reactions. When we first land in the States, I find myself making worldly judgments on pretty much anything that moves. Life is simple in China. American culture is so fast and so pre-occupied with being cool, that being cynical is actually really easy.

You choose to see the waste of throwing out three-dozen bagels after the store has closed because the Health Department demands it. You notice how many times we look in mirrors and concern ourselves with outward beauty. Your mind reels at the advertising of low-riding jeans to eight-year old girls and it all makes you want to leave the country and find a dark musky monastery to hide your children in. The hardest part about all of it is that the people around you don't notice anymore, like when a baker ceases to notice the incredible smell of a chocolate cake baking. The smells and features around you just become irrelevant background noise. It's not always a horrible thing, it just happens.

So, when you pipe up and make comments about how quiet things are in America or how many choices there are in the mall food court, your courteous friend will nod but won't really understand what you're talking about. When you try to tell them what a street vendor would sell you for breakfast, they won't get it and they might even say "That's weird." A few years ago, you also would have thought it was weird, but now it's home. Now it's real to you and it hurts when people don't understand- when people don't want to understand. It's ok for *you* to pick on China, but not for others to regard it as strange, similar to you picking on a little brother.

In order to tell a simple story about something that happened to you at dinner, you have to explain how a Chinese restaurant works. There are rules about placing your chopsticks, tea kettles that need pouring at ritually appropriate times, waiters who stand there and tell you that you will need to pick something else because you've already ordered two dishes with potatoes. At each table, there are large Lazy Susans that require precise timing to turn, while loud parties around you smoke and clank beer bottles together. Then, there's a bill at the end of the meal that shouldn't be divided right there in the middle of the restaurant. In order for your story to make any sort of sense, our friends need these textures to fill in the picture of what a dinnertime might look like. But once you realize all of this, you end up just not telling the story. It's too hard to communicate and if you are honest, you aren't totally sure the other person wants to know. Many times, as you start to tell a China story, there is a certain glaze that sweeps over your friend's eyes. You might as well be talking about the baby you birthed that sprouted wings because they are nodding in agreement, but not at all listening.

But there is always that one family that understands. That one group of friends that love you enough to invite you over for BBQ and let you tell the story about the time your daughter pointed through the split pants at a little boy's "package" and how it mortified you. But then you laughed with your neighbor and now you are friends. Or about the first month you were in China and tried out a new Chinese phrase by accidentally telling a local vendor that you wanted to buy a daughter instead of milk. There is always someone who cares about how much you love using chopsticks and the smell of fried dumplings in the night market. One of the first things we do when we land in the States is find those people and invite ourselves over to their homes. We bring pictures, snacks, memories, and parts of our lives that get tucked away when we try to become "normal" Americans for a few months. We treasure those people dearly because they care about us deeply. They care not just about the adventures we have while living overseas, but they care about our marriage and parenting. They care about *us*.

We only visit the States every 3-4 years. China is home. We have to remind people of that when they come up to us and ask if it's nice to be "home." America is no longer our home. As a Christian, this world is not my home. After having lived in China for almost seven years now, we are still reminded daily of how we are aliens and strangers in this country and on this earth. We are to stay alert and aware of everything, as if it's new and strange, like a child who happens upon a ladybug for the first time. No matter how long we live in China, we will never be insiders; we will never completely fit in. We should never grow comfortable in our earthly skin because we've been fit into a new creation.

A butterfly need not grow jealous of the confines of a caterpillar just because the caterpillar can easily camouflage against the leaves of a tree. The step of a caterpillar is clumsy and slow. Their days are filled with eating and lopping along in the dirt. But all the while, the little guy is being prepared for a task that is greater. A task that includes dancing through the air with sun kissed wings; a flight that lands him on cherry red snapdragons; a night's rest on a bundle of fennel bushes. All of these things seem ridiculous to a meager caterpillar, because he only sees a slinky brown exterior with padded feet. Imagining a life of flowers and flight is foolish. I often feel like that caterpillar. I just want to blend in and hide behind the safety of a tree. I don't want to stick out or be different just because I live in China. But that's not what God has for my family or for me. I so easily forget that I am created to be different and that because of our life calling, there is grace in each day as I am reminded that I don't belong here.

## things to remember upon arrival in america

I was fairly nervous about what life would look like for us in America. While having grown up there, we had been gone for several years now. I tried to think of all our various spheres of life and all the things we needed to remember if we wanted to try and fit in. For example:

Americans wear deodorant and expect you to do the same.
Women shave their legs.
People change clothes and bathe more than twice a week.
If you have a congested nose, it is not ok to hold your finger on one nostril and blow the contents out the other.
They expect ice in their cold drinks.
Toilet paper is not an appropriate substitute for a napkin or a coffee filter.
Pushing your way to the cashier is not the definition of "standing in line."
Everyone in my vicinity will now understand people-watching observations said in English.
Most Americans don't use their car horns to warn other drivers that they are coming.
Red lights actually mean stop.
Having random people take my children's picture with their personal phones is not normal.

I will have to explain to my kids kickball, frozen foods, parades, and Justin Bieber.

*parasites are gross*

We had planned on doing a three-month stay in America until we discovered that our daughter Joi was having issues with her blood. Over two years ago, we brought home a curious, shy one-year old girl from Ethiopia and it changed our lives forever. Apart from a minor bout with scabies, we have had very little medical issues with her. That was until we had a physical done, revealing that part of her white blood cell count was at a dangerously high level. The probable diagnosis was allergies, parasites, or leukemia. We were obviously hoping for the first.

Funny how we think that our plans are so perfect and worked out until God gets a hold of them and writes over all of it in His huge red Sharpie. Crossing out words and dates. Editing out numbers and figures. But then He hands our plans back to us, edited in His handwriting and at the top writes "Perfect." Every one of our kids came to America with parasites.

When American doctors pull out their clipboards and begin asking questions about my children's diet, I always start to laugh. They ask questions like: "Have your children eaten any meat cooked in a non-hygienic environment?" Or, "Do you eat any meats other than chicken, pork or beef?" I gently remind them that I live in China and that half the time I'm not even sure we are actually eating meat. I go on to tell them that we eat food from street vendors that have mangy dogs circling their legs and sweet children that haven't bathed in months handing us our food. They patiently put down their clipboards and sigh.

My time in America has shown me that Americans feel that parasites are indeed quite disgusting-and I apparently have lost my filter in some areas. When people ask about why we are extending our stay here, I tell them: "Our kids have worms." This sentence is usually met with a small shriek and a look like they've just seen their grandparents naked. Worms and intestinal issues are a daily part of our family life in China.

Many times, our evening routine begins with "Mommy, there are worms dancing in the toilet!" "Ok," I reply, "don't flush, I'll be right there to look." Then I look and take a mental picture before rushing to the computer and Googling "intestinal worms/parasites." I would suggest staying with the "apple pie recipe" Google search because the "intestinal worms" search brings up images that make you gag involuntarily and maybe throw up in your mouth a little. This has become so normal for us living overseas that I find myself now in America and talking about it with Tammie, the bank teller and the guy selling fried rice at Moon Wok Café.

I have to research these worms because I want to make sure that the worms dancing in the toilet are not deadly. That the worms paying us a visit will eventually get bored and leave my kids' systems. There is really no way around getting worms in our lifestyle. We don't ever know where the food is coming from, how the meat got to the market, what kinds of wonderful delights the street vendors might pass along, or even what type of meat we are actually serving at our dinner table. With all of these unknowns, our little "Name that Parasite" game will have to remain a constant part of our day. But I am learning now when people ask me why we are still in America, I simply reply, "Our children have some medical issues."

## illogical people everywhere

I'm sitting here by myself among sepia toned shadows cast from moonlit windows because the electricity is out. I didn't think this kind of thing happened in America. It's funny the utopian like qualities that we attribute to living in America. In China, we have grown accustomed to electricity going out. As a matter of fact, ours goes out daily. Daily because we use almost triple the amount of electricity as everyone else in the building. Every few months, the electric bill is posted on the front door of our building for everybody to look at and scrutinize. We try to sneak down with a marker and cross ours out, even if we haven't paid it yet so that nobody can see how much we owe. Or we rip off a piece of our numbers so that it looks like some punk kid was messing with it. It's all very mature.

We are usually mortified at how much more our electricity is compared to everyone else in the building. Every few months after the bill posting fiasco, I vow to try and lower our costs. I then remember that we have a family of seven. So the markers and petty vandalism continue. The Chinese are very good at conservation. Many friends of ours have air conditioners that they refuse to turn on and lights they leave dark because they want to save money on electricity.

Our first week back in the States, I was in my parent's pantry which has an automatic light that goes off when the door is closed. I was in there looking for something processed that I could cook in 90 seconds and feed my five ravenous wolves. All of the sudden, the lights went out and I said (in Chinese), "Ah, our electricity went out." And then a revelation of industrial proportions went off in my head: We're in America! Electricity doesn't go out here. I literally had that thought run through my head, as if America had bought the patent to eternal electricity and was hording the rights from the rest of the world.

When we landed in the States this last time, I was fairly fed up with Chinese culture. I know that I am supposed to love it everyday. I know that I am supposed to want to listen to Beijing Opera and eat pigs ears for breakfast, but ya know what…it's just not like that for me all the time. I do have my days where I enjoy making dumplings with families in their non-kid friendly homes. And I have my days where the grandmothers and their criticisms don't affect me. But there are more than a few days that I get tired and frustrated and want to throw my rice bowl on the floor in a completely inappropriate temper tantrum.

One of the cultural frustrations that often catches me is what I perceive as illogical thinking. See I assumed, being the good American that I am, that all Chinese were good at math and science. Growing up, all the smart kids were named Wang or Lee. Chinese kids dominated the science fairs by inventing super conducting magnetic railways from paper clips and rubber bands. I would sit with my experiment of a baking soda volcano and the Chinese kids would be backing their experiments in on a semi. It's just the way things work in the States. We've all come to expect it. Kind of like loss of bladder control after birthing 4 babies. You adjust your expectations and your activities. Like eliminating jumping jacks. Forever. In the same way, you plan on getting 2nd or 3rd place at the science fair. You expect to get the lower grade on the math test. With all of this cultural baggage in tow, I arrived in China expecting five-year olds to be surveying land and finding cures for cancer at playtime.

I have actually found the opposite to be true. The thinking patterns here are usually not logical nor systematic. For example, we've been told by several young college students that they know that God doesn't exist. They have certifiable proof. They proceed to tell us that God doesn't exist because men and women have the same number of ribs. You see, if God took a rib from Adam and formed Eve, then men should have one less rib than women. And some of them believe this logic. We then ask them "If you cut off your finger and then have a baby, how many fingers will your baby have?" "10 fingers," they reply. "That's right," we try to answer without sounding patronizing and expressing the thoughts that are really going through our heads. "You would have 10 fingers because it doesn't matter if you lose a finger. Your DNA is set for 10 fingers." And with that, they look at us with intellectual amazement that we were able to punch a hole right through their airtight argument against God.

I'm not saying Chinese people are dumb. They are smarter in different ways. Most of them just aren't strong in logic. I was not at all expecting that. Then, after the first week here in the States, I was driving back home and from the corner of my eye I saw a busted fire hydrant spewing water at break neck speeds. Six inches in front of the spewing water sat an innocent little bucket. A bucket to catch Niagara Falls. I chuckled. I reminded myself that illogical people exist everywhere, even in America. And it made me miss China.

## being not busy

It's interesting being in the States, because I am reminded of the standard greeting that goes something like this: "Hey, how you doing?" "Oh man, I'm good, but busy. Yeah, it's been a crazy week." This happens almost every time. I catch myself using it as my default answer. Then I think back on my week and say to myself, "Why did I say that? I wasn't terribly busy. And things weren't any more crazy than they are in a normal week in our home." But if I said "It was good; not much really went on; pretty relaxed, actually." People would look at me in outward jealousy, but their inner monologue would sound like this: "What a loser. Do they not have anything productive to do with their time? They must not have anyone vying for their attention, which means that they must not have much value as a person." I know this because I find myself having these thoughts about others. I hate it. I know it's wrong and I'm trying to change.

My identity cannot be based on how busy or productive I am. It cannot be valued based on how many people need me or want my attention on something, because realistically, we could all be replaced. Probably by someone with more talent and expertise than we have to offer. When my satisfaction lies solely in Christ and not others, my joy overflows from morning to dusk. When I remove myself from the race of this world and rest in Jesus, it's the most satisfying thing I have experienced. The Chinese are really good at valuing their time with people. They will come over and hang out all afternoon because you are more important than any task that could be manufactured. I am jealous of their contentment with the simple. I am envious of their satisfaction in sitting and silence. Even in conversations, the average long pause among my Chinese friends could be minutes. The awkward pause drives us Americans crazy. We feel naked and insecure, like Junior High kids in the locker room. So we fill that space. Sometimes we will even cough or itch or make an obvious observation about the weather, just to fill the silent corners in conversation.

I want to learn from my Chinese friends how to just *be*. Not doing, not producing… just being. I've always had a hard time with the Mary and Martha story in the Bible for this exact reason. I've always been frustrated by this story because it seemed like Mary was being lazy and Martha was being a dutiful host. And then China happened. China-where our Christian brothers and sisters want nothing more than a musky room and a dim light to read their Bibles by. Where they want to sit by Jesus' feet so that they can hang onto every comma and exclamation mark in the Bible. Meanwhile, I, in all my 'American-ness', tend to slave away in the kitchen trying to 'do' for Jesus. And more times than not, I miss Him. I miss what Jesus is trying to say amidst the clamoring of my pots and pans. I completely and totally miss Him.

## tight community

One of the things that was different for us when we visited America was the neighborhoods. As we walked around our suburban dwellings, people for the most part stayed within the confines of their own personal kingdoms. In the neighborhood that we were living in, there were front gates to most of the homes acting as a closed drawbridge to the outside community. Several times I thought about bringing things to our neighbors but then realized that throwing chocolate chips cookies over their fence like a Sunday newspaper would probably not be received well. So we ducked our heads back into our shells and didn't meet many neighbors.

The few times that we did interact with them, it was through the bars of the fence. Our fences of independence have actually just made us prisoners of self-inflicted loneliness. The unfortunate part was that the longer we lived there, the more I grew to like the separation. I would dodge an interaction at the mailbox or avoid eye contact while picking up the morning's newspaper. I became accustomed to mingling with the community that I had already chosen rather than interacting with any strangers that the Lord might have directed to cross my path. So many of us treat real community like a game of kickball and we are all a bunch of skinny introverted kids just waiting to be invited to play. While we all want to play, we are also nervous that if we actually get invited in, we will end up flat on our backs, muddy and with a bloody nose. And you know what, sometimes being in community is that way. It's messy, bloody, and makes you look like an idiot. But at least you are playing.

Our home in China is always in community. Our apartment is only one of thousands in this complex. The buildings tower over me to remind me that I am but one small piece of this communal structure built around me. Every time I go outside, people are there. If I am out of town for a day, everybody knows. Each time my footsteps want to quicken to avoid people, I am stopped by a neighbor asking me if all these children are mine. I am forced to slow my independence. On several occasions, we have spotted entire families sitting at their window's ledge watching us foreigners eat dinner. When my husband has ulcers, the neighbor brings down crushed watermelon rind to aid the healing process because she knows what is orbiting in our world. I know when our neighbor's son is finished with his English lessons because we bump into them in the elevator. Living in this type of community has reminded me that to really love those around us, we need to know what it is that is around them. We need to be aware of their daily struggles and victories. While that is easy for me to do with friends, it's also important for me to engage strangers in that same way. Living in this apartment complex forces my independence into submission to loving strangers and allowing my world to be expanded by including those around me.

Another aspect of community is our relationship with other foreigners. In each city we have lived in here, there have been about 20 other non-Chinese friends for us to get to know. There are times that flying together with my foreign friends, like desperate moths to a light, seems the only rational thing to do. On those "bad China days," you look to other foreigners who can tell you similar stories of confusion and frustration. Many of these people are completely opposite me in personality, but we come together because they understand me when I talk about my 8th grade crush on A.C. Slater or the time I asked for a Jennifer Aniston haircut and ended up looking like Blossom.

Then there are those foreigners who are fortunate enough to be brought here by some large engineering company. They invite us poor pithy foreigners over for dinner and feed us steak made from real cows. Despite personality differences, there is comfort in knowing that there are a few people who understand how you think and where you have been.

### things I love about texans

1. They wear scarves like accessories. I just saw a girl with a tank top and 2 scarves. Those who have actually lived in the cold know that scarves are no joking matter.
2. All soft drinks are called "Coke" and they are poured into in cups at least the size of your thigh. When ordering in a restaurant in Texas, you say "I want a large Coke," to which the waiter replies "What kind?" And you usually answer with, "Dr. Pepper."
3. Texans like to hunt all types of living creatures. And they will bark at each other as if it's a sport to sit in a big stand and shoot the creatures that have been trained to come to that exact spot and eat corn. If you hunt with a bow and arrow, I will grant you the word "sport." If it's with a gun and a feed stand, I'm gonna have to call a spade a spade....you are doing a drive-by on a deer.
4. Texans put bumper stickers on their cars that talk about guns, being a Republican, and expressing their right to secede from the Union.
5. We feel sorry for real Mexican food because it's infinitely inferior to Tex-Mex.
6. We talk about football like it's a matter of life and death. And we tell our sons to man-up. All of this is in hope that one day they will become big tough football players and buy their mamas a home.
7. Allowing your infant child to take their first sip of Dr. Pepper is a rite of passage. This is usually done by the father and is secretly endorsed by the mother because publicly, she doesn't give her child caffeine.

8. We complain when it dips beneath 32 degrees because we don't know how to drive in freezing weather. So we cancel school, stay home from work and buy canned beans so we can hunker down for the night.

9. Texans wear boots all year round. We accessorize with belts made of rattlesnake and oversized buckles that have the initials KT on it. We then make up for it in our undersized jeans that lead to blood clots in our shins.

## Wal-Mart Bliss

Wal-Mart, oh Wal-Mart what do I say?
The feelings and emotions I want to convey.

Your blue and white sign lure me right
to your front door like a moth to the light.

As I walk I am struck by the people around
the mullets and pajama pants abundantly abound.

I try to focus on the pretzels and bread
but I am distracted by the lady with fruit on her head.

Many people are wearing shorts that are riding
in places where skin should rather be hiding.

The prices are low, the items are cheap
but is it safe for me to enter, is it safe for me to creep?

I like it best to shop fairly late,
Why do your prices all end in 98?

As I walk briskly to my car each Monday
I am escorted by Rick in his security Hyundai.

And my Chinese friends are forever grateful
for the jobs that I realize make Americans hateful.

Wal-Mart, oh Wal-Mart you make my life easy
even if your store makes me feel kinda queasy.

## systematically praying for hollywood

The idolization of actors, athletes, and rock stars is not something I have missed by living overseas. The amount of time the media spends on following the lives of these people is staggering. While floods and famines are happening around the world, a large part of the population is concerned with what Brad Pitt likes on his hamburger. I have never been one to go weak at the knees when I saw a celebrity, actually I have always felt sorry for them. As a child, I used to spend a lot of time organizing my tapes. For those of you under 30, that's the way we all used to listen to music. We would record things off the radio and make mixtapes for our friends… and sometimes for the boys we had crushes on. Then we would write I love ----, with each space representing a letter of his name on our Trapper Keepers. It was very mature and very real for all of us. This was also very convenient when we changed our minds the next week. We could just add a letter or two so that we could change the name to our new love.

Back to the tape organization. I would arrange my tapes so that the non-Christian tapes would sit right next to my Christian tapes. So it looked like this: Michael Jackson, Petra, Madonna, DC Talk, Poison, Michael W. Smith. Then I prayed for those Christian tapes to have a good influence on my non-Christian tapes. As if, like "Night at the Museum," Sandi Patti would start evangelizing to George Michael at night while I slept. I totally believed this would work and I thought I was a genius for thinking of the idea. Please feel free to steal this idea. I know it will transform the world. I was sure of it then and I'm sure of it now.

## fly in my coffee

Just now, a fly pranced around the edge of my mug for a good two minutes before plunging deep into the abyss of my coffee.

The curious fly probably smelled the peppermint creamer I had laced my black coffee with and couldn't help but try and taste it. He had no idea that waiting at the bottom of my mug was his definite demise. He simply wanted a quick taste. My little fly friend could have stayed up on the edge of my cup and probably tasted remnants of the creamer that had dusted the top when I poured it in. But it wanted more. The smells were stronger at the bottom. The delights to be had became more and more enticing the further in he dove. It wanted what would ultimately lead to its struggle and eventual death.

Now I look at this little fly floating lifelessly at the bottom of my porcelain mug. His taste was enjoyed for a mere second or two before he drowned. This is what sin does to us...to me. I think that it will satisfy. Just one little sip won't really matter. But what starts out as naive curiosity and an act of impulsive rebellion will end in my own demise. So often these days, sin is categorized as pride or pornography. Yeah, yeah, we're all prideful. And we know that pornography rips people apart. But the sins of laziness, impatience or ingratitude get tucked nicely away into the pockets of nominal sin. "They aren't really that hurtful," we repeat in order to pacify our itching ears.

In the same light, taking a little taste of the peppermint creamer on my mug wasn't hurtful to the fly. At first. But once we have a taste of sin, our appetites seem to grow and it's at that point that we commit to diving into the deep. Usually we don't even realize we are diving until we splash down into sin and struggle to find our way to the surface again. We end up in a tailspin of vertigo, no longer able to tell which way is up. I have to pray for strength to avoid the mug altogether. I don't even need to fly around it, gazing boldfaced at temptation. I need to fly past and find a tree branch on which to land or a pile of crackers to devour. God didn't create flies with the ability to swim. He created them to fly, land, and annoy us at picnics. When we become children of the Lord, we are created to soar past sin knowing that the joys to be had in Christ give us freedom to fly.

# Moving in with Uncle Sam

"For through him we both have access in one Spirit
to the Father. So then you are no longer strangers
and aliens, but you are fellow citizens with the saints
and members of the household of God."

Ephesians 2:18-19 (ESV)

*With Joi's blood work still in limbo, we decided to settle into American life a little. We would not be returning to China until we had received full medical clearance. Knowing this, I took a long-term perspective by renewing my vows with limeade slushies and waffle fries.*

## fighting scrub demons

Back and forth to the hospital in downtown Houston, my heart and head became stuck in the traffic jam of the unknown. I began to get angry with the entire medical profession for not having a clue what was wrong. I found myself honking my horn at people while driving recklessly to the hospital just to make myself feel vindicated. So I wrote a few things down instead of venting steam on the poor guy at Jiffy Lube. Because one way or another, I needed to burn some anxious energy. Obviously.

*January 22, 2010*

*Jackson has been out of town now for 21 days as he begins his PhD seminars. Today I had to take Joi for yet another blood test. She has had blood drawn almost a dozen times in the 18 months that she's been home. Because she was born in Ethiopia, adopted, and then brought straight to China, the doctor's are at a loss in pinpointing one out of the thousands of possible parasites that could be plaguing her little body. The sight of a person in scrubs makes her climb up into my arms and cling to me as if she could actually hide inside my skin. We can be in Subway and she will see a nurse walk in and she starts to cry. She will never be a doctor, nor will she marry a doctor, nor will she go to the doctor as an adult.*

*A tornado of anxiety has been whirling around my stomach for the three hours before her blood was even taken. The results from this blood test will determine whether or not we go back overseas. It's like the 'Showcase Showdown' for blood work. This scares me. It scares me because I can't do anything about it. And the thought of not living in China and not doing what we are doing makes me forget to breathe. I don't even have the emotional energy to put down on paper what I feel. I'm fighting to trust the Lord. He has been generously faithful to our family. He has shown me things over the last few weeks that tell me that we will return overseas in about a month and a half. But sometimes I feel juvenile when I say, "I KNOW what God is going to do in this situation." Probably because I am just nervous that I'll be wrong and then I'll look like a moron. I am choosing to trust these gracious signs that the Lord has dropped in my path. I am going to receive them as signs of our eventual return to China.*

*A small yellow piece of paper inscribed with her blood results will tell us what our future will look like. These results will remind me that God is God no matter what happens in our day. And then the day after tomorrow, Jackson comes home. I wish he were here to listen to the results with me. I wish he were here to feel the weight of these tests. He is as concerned as I am; he is just far away. When you are far away, you get the luxury of disconnecting a little from the impact of the punches.*

The next few days would be wrought with prayer, anxiety and more than a few nervous digestion issues. I trusted the Lord with the outcome of these results, but physically my body was wearying from the fight. Those 48 hours between getting the blood drawn and the nurse calling seemed to take 96 hours. It was as if each painful minute mocked me as it slowly crept back up to the 12. I sat there and stared at the clock on the microwave until it hit 8:30 a.m. At that point, I could reach a nurse who could read me the results.

*January 24, 2010*

*As I was waiting endlessly for the nurse to call me with the results, I was thinking of excuses to call the nurse myself. Certainly some child of mine had a sudden rash or if I rubbed their foreheads with enough fervor, I'm sure we could feign a fever. Finally, I broke through all semblance of self-control and called our nurse, Linda. Linda was with a patient. After all the wrangling I did with my hoodie as I waited, the nurse called me back and reported that her blood was back to normal! I sank into the plush yellow chair in my parent's living room, cried a little and then rejoiced.*

## my little gum infatuation

As Wal-Mart became a regular part of my weekly routine, I found myself sucked into the "Mommy please" aisle. That's the aisle where rowdy kids wear their mothers down by asking for all the insulin nightmares that are waiting for them at the end of the shopping trip. All you want to do is throw your money at the cashier and get into your air conditioned car, and then some genius marketing agent in L.A. decided it was a good idea to stack candy and gum into a nice little display to officially push you over the edge of sanity. But, one day, I spotted a special on Extra gum. The company started a line of these dessert gums. It changed my life. So much so, that I wrote a poem about my little summer fling.

## Gum Infatuation

I never thought, I never knew
What life was like before there was you.

But one day I spotted to the left there did sit,
My newfound friend named "Mint Chocolate Chip"

I realize our friendship is shallow and new,
But from the very first bite, I simply knew.

We are friends forever like Michel W said.
Thoughts of your leaving, I dare not tread.

You are consistent and sweet and loyal and true
You add skip to my step, make my skies blue.

Some might say my feelings are dumb
But I say it's fine to be in love with your gum.

As a final display of my undying devotion, I bought eight packs of mint chocolate chip gum to bring back with me to China. If the kids ask me to share, I will say no.

## suburbia strangulation

I grew up in a middle class planned community north of Houston, Texas. This is where we have been living while visiting the States. When you grow up in a planned community, you learn that there are rules. Rules that tell you what color to paint your basketball goal, the time of day to bring your trash can back to the house, what kind of car is acceptable to drive and the tax bracket in which you should fall. The McDonald's signs can only be waist high and the Sonic drive-thrus are stacked in matching earth tone brick. There is an order. And that order has been set on its course since the planned community's non-accidental conception. There is nothing wham bam thank you ma'am about it. Growing up, my family used to receive these indiscreet little letters from the planned community Nazis telling us that if our trashcan wasn't put in our garage by Thursday, they were going to fine us. Or take away our middle-class ID card. Most certainly they would send out their hawks to swarm our house every week until the problem was rectified. I vowed to find these people a hobby.

More time and concern was spent maintaining this code than actually living. Families built sound, color-appropriate pillars to hold up their shanty house lives. Many of the inside structures of the families I knew were in shambles, but on the outside there was a gloss of expensive lacquer that held the whole structure together. Both husband and wife would trudge to meetings late into the night so that their children could drive a Porsche at sixteen. It all seemed so distant to me.

I never really desired to be super trendy. My grandmother's homemade hammer pants were just fine by my standards, but I sat among the chaos of others and it seemed to swirl about making everyone dizzy. Yet everyone still kept a watchful eye on the progress of those in their circles. Like when you watch a ballerina spin, she always focuses on a spot. The spot is not only the thing that keeps her up straight, but it's also the thing that keeps her from allowing the circling disorientation to consume her. That spot for most of the people I knew was called reputation.

When I was a child, I would sit in church, and wonder what people would do if a homeless person walked in and sat in the prized fourth row. Nobody except the preacher's grandmother and the pitied Scripture reader sat in the front row. The fourth row was safe. No eye contact with the preacher, no leading of the communion line. I spent dozens of Sundays coming up with a plan to walk in disguised as a homeless person. I would walk with a limp, because homeless people always had ankle problems in my world. My dress would be dirty and ragged and I would smell like boiled liver. On my eyes, I would be wearing sunglasses to disguise my real identity. I'd probably have to pretend I was blind so as to justify my wearing sunglasses in a softly lit room. This contrived little game in my head never ended well for my church friends. I envisioned them taking me by the collar and escorting me passed the marbled fountains and framed crossed-stitched Jesus looking like Fabio, to end up in the atrium alone. My mind was in a constant race to outwit suburbia. I got tired of the sameness. Realistically, the only time I saw someone who looked different than me was when I went to the roller skating rink. Or Wal-Mart after 10 pm.

My mom has always been very put together and well mannered. She didn't even like it when we tipped the waitress at Marco's Mexican Food that it was her birthday so that they could come out to sing Feliz Cumpleaños and cram an overworn sombrero on her head. I'm not sure how she came to birth a first-born girl who hated all things about growing up in any sort of formal manner. I maintained this sort of life outlook up until they could hand me over to my poor husband on our wedding day. I eagerly suggested having a do-it-yourself burrito buffet at our wedding reception. The same wedding reception that was to be held inside a fancy resort conference room. I don't even think my mom let me fully explain the plan I had dreamt up before coughing, smiling politely, and changing the topic to something more benign like her new herb garden. Despite having a loving home, tennis courts around the corner and trashcans identical to the rest of the neighborhood, I felt like a butterfly squirming around in a cocoon. My wings felt like they were contorted unnaturally down by my side. I never quite wore suburbia well.

As a senior in high school, my freshman sister would make me drop her off at the curb so that she could walk in by herself. My high school attire consisted of sweats or whatever I wore for pajamas the night before, a wet head and a backpack. I was an athlete and had not a care in the world what anyone thought of me. Which actually translated into having a huge issue with people pleasing and desire for people to take notice. But I wasn't going to let people in on that.

My parents can thankfully attest that I've always been given at least one friend who was my 'voice of reason.' See, I'm a rather impulsive person and so if I felt like buying soup to carry around in my car so that I could pretend to throw up at stop lights, or strap a college roommate's pet turtle to a parachute and send it para-trooping off our balcony, I would at least have a friend around to tell me I was a moron. I didn't always listen, but those people kept me out of more trouble than I had coming to me. I was always that girl at the slumber parties that stuck girls' hands in hot water or filled open drooling mouths with toothpaste. On behalf of all of you that have horrible slumber party memories, I am sorry. I was indeed one of 'those' girls.

I was a gymnast up until ninth grade, so that brought a few dynamics into play. First was that I would hit puberty later than all my friends. This would force me to have to lie when asked if I had any products to borrow when in the locker room. I would just shrug my shoulders and tell them it wasn't my time of the month or that I forgot them in my purse. I actually had no idea what they were talking about. My mom had never talked to me about these girly issues and I made M.A.S.H. puzzles while we had that talk at school in fourth grade. Certainly finding out if I was going to live in a mansion with my 13 kids was more interesting than whatever girly things they were showing on that video.

The other little gift that gymnastics brought me was the lack of need to wear a bra. While I had a killer six-pack, most junior high girls don't actually want that six pack to make its way up to their shoulders. I had nothing. But at recess, the boys popped our bras and I had only a flapping shirt, so I decided that I needed to fix that little misunderstanding quickly. I told my mom that I was blossoming and that I should get a bra. Unfortunately, there was no blossoming actually happening. As a matter of fact, the seeds weren't planted, no watering was needed and certainly no sprouts were poking through the soil. But I couldn't bear the humiliation of a pop-free shirt. I got the bra. Then stuffed it. After settling that, I threw on my jelly bracelets, set my teased bangs solid with hair spray and headed to the bus stop. I then spent all day retrieving said bra from up around my neck. You see, when you wear an undergarment with nothing to hold it down, things slide. I must have pulled that thing down 57 times that day. But come recess time all that faded to gray, when the boys came by and found a little something to pop. Mission accomplished.

It was at this point that I remember realizing that I just never seemed on the front end of the trendy curve. I always seemed to be late to realize that things were in and out of style. I never cared about going to parties just so I could show off the embarrassing pictures on Monday morning. None of this made sense to me. And now we are raising our kids in a city so foreign to America suburbia that I find myself wandering around with my shoulders up by my ears in utter cluelessness. The smells, sounds, sights, struggles are all different. I'm sure my kids will grow up craving less noise, more order, smells that don't resemble sweaty, garlicky feet and they will move to the American suburbs. Things always seem to full circle that way.

## speaking chinese

It's funny when people in America discover that you can speak Chinese, or at least you could speak Chinese seven months ago when you left. They always want you to say something, to which our children teach the unsuspecting strangers elementary school inappropriate phrases to say in Chinese. They slowly pronounce and teach them, "I love to pass gas!" They think it's hilarious and laugh under their straight faces as they watch the poor adult say "I LOVE to pass gas" over and over again in delight because now they are speaking Chinese. And then I have to pretend to discipline them because that's what a responsible mother is supposed to do.

People want us to do one of three things when they learn that we can speak Chinese. They either want us to translate words so they can get them tattooed on their bodies; pick an exotic character out to put on their youth group retreat advertisement; or take you to their nail place to have a conversation with Kim, their Vietnamese nail lady.

Since being in the States, we have heard a few funny stories of people getting Chinese tattooed on their bodies incorrectly. My favorite so far is the poor young girl who thought she was getting "Christ is Lord" tattooed on the nape of her neck. In order to get the most authentic tattoo possible, she went into Chinatown and found a Chinese tattoo artist. She had wonderfully romantic notions of bringing entire lost tribes to salvation through her little tattoo, overlooking the fact that whisking your long blonde locks up off your neck and exposing your tattoo is rather inappropriate in a conservative part of the country where the women don't even wear pants. She got strange looks every time she had people read her tattoo and after several weeks of receiving perplexing reactions she decided to ask around. At the end of her perilous pursuit she discovered the unfortunate news that the word "Chrysler" had been permanently inked on the back of her neck, not "Christ is Lord." While the tattoo artist's Chinese characters were authentic and lovely, his English was not. So when he heard "Christ is Lord", his ears told him "Chrysler."

### My Gas Station Poem

When I came to the States, I dared and I dreamed
Of cheese on my sandwich but with bread not steamed.

And quickly I found my newest infatuation
It's not cheese or ice, it's the American gas station.

Today I walked in and my what did my eyes lay hold
But rabbit poop ice keeping my Dr. Pepper cold.

I felt the sky open as I added the cherry,
Flavoring no doubt to make you skip and be merry.

Then I turned to the rotating sausage and dogs
And wondered how many organs would be clogged

By the spinning wienies toasted Hollywood brown.
But, I skipped those for now and headed around,

The crusty kolaches with that halo of grease
Corn nuts and those elusive Boston Baked Beans.

It's almost too much for my mind to take in.
My eyes all atwinkle, I don't know where to begin.

Fried Pork Rinds taunting 0 grams of carbs
I'm so glad that's good for my Atkins and heart.

Wash them down with a 64 oz cup of caffeine.
With more choices of gum than should ever be seen.

I chat with the cashier and think to myself
What's with the clipboard? Are you counting the shelves?

But I will tell you that walking through those doors,
Keeps my heart beating to come back for more.

The hot dogs, the candy, the oversized Coke.
The people inside, the blogs they provoke.

If I could just pump the gas all would be dandy
Besides, gas in my car sure would be handy.

It seems I've forgotten the gas pumping way
The lift, the push, what's there to say?

But it seems I can't do it, that simple ol' chore
So I grunt at the pump and open my door.

Hoping tomorrow will be a success
Cause I'm needing gas, so on I will press!

On Shell, on Mobil, on Valero and Racetrack
Tomorrow is new and tomorrow I'll be back

## texas "winters"

Texas winters are the best. We mockingly call the cold fronts that are scattered throughout December, January and February "winter." In between those mild little cold fronts is warmth. We don't confine our flip-flops or khaki shorts to the closet to wait for summer. Sometimes we can even go water skiing in February. The funniest thing though is to watch Texans fake their way through winter. We turn on our air conditioners so that we can have a fire, and we sit next to it with our wool afghans that grandma crocheted for our wedding gift. We drink hot chocolate next to said fire and talk about how tomorrow it might dip down into the 40's, so we'd better cover the pipes and drape the bushes. It's fantastic, really.

People pull out fur coats and scarves and wear them to the grocery store because the air conditioner is still on inside. Then we camp out extra long in the frozen foods section and declare how grateful we are to have such a warm coat that we could wear today. On days that it actually drops below 35 degrees, schools will cancel classes and businesses will close their doors for the day. Nobody is prepared to drive in the ice, and mass chaos ensues because Texans don't know how to survive in the cold.

We throw on scarves over our tank tops and go out for a drive in our convertible VW Bug to watch the kids' choir sing Christmas carols at the mall. Churches will even bring in machines that cover their parking lots in fake snow so that kids can trample around in it and throw pretend snowballs. And that is our winter. Most of the roses will make it till spring and I'll be picking peppers out of my parent's garden to make salsa for Christmas dinner.

I remember wearing my coveted letter jacket in high school starting in October. I was so proud of those chunky red letters touting all my glorious accomplishments. No way I was missing out on wearing that thing just because Texas weather wouldn't indulge in my narcissistic wardrobe. I remember wearing it with my shorts. And sweating. Lots. But I didn't care. I swear the jacket glowed when I hung it back up in my closet.

## *why I love coffee shops*

I love coffee shops. Or any public place that has free Internet, coffee and a bathroom within running distance. While the coffee is what gets me here, it's the people that make me stay. Take the two middle-aged women on my right. From the moment the woman in the polyester coat walked in, they have been talking about her recent hair change in hair color. Just now, Gary walked around the corner. He must be the son of the woman in the black, flower-embroidered coat. There was squealing and arbitrary laughter as each member of their party swung open the doors and let in the cold.

An older man just sat down not even 24 inches away from me. He's straining as he works on those arduous crosswords opposite the comics in the daily newspaper. I used to pretend to be smart enough to conquer the crossword. I wised up at a young age and would wait until the next day's answers came out and I'd fill them in. It helped me feel closure and victory. But why did he sit so close to me even though there are five or six tables open behind him?

He has now fallen asleep. What is it with old people and falling asleep at random? I used to beat my grandmother at Parcheesi from this simple act of nature alone.

Maybe it's that I'm sitting in the purple plush seats broken in by the thousands of customers who have sat here before me. There is history in these chairs; break-ups, make-ups, job interviews, college searches, father/son talks, and marriage dreams. More than these lovely chairs, I think it's that this older gentleman with his Korean War medal pinned to his striped cardigan, wants to feel a part of a group. He desires, like all of us, to know and to be known. It's why we obsess over our number count on our Facebook page. It's why we inwardly sulk when there's a "0 comments" tag line at the end of a heartfelt blog. It's why we sometimes pretend to be looking at our phones checking on some type of urgent matter while standing in line. It's the idea that being known makes us valuable that throws a net over our ability to thrive.

In America, to be unknown is to have failed. For me, the times that this becomes most overwhelming are when I diminish the fact of being known by the Creator of all things good.

Our God is the God that whispers wind through fall yellows and reds; the God that takes cells and from them produces a soul; the God that takes foul brown beans, soaks them in water, calls it coffee and declares…it is good!; it is that very God that has cloaked His children with garments of salvation and covered us with the robe of righteousness (Isa. 10). That should be satisfying enough to us that we would never have to check our number counts or fake text again. He should be enough. He is enough.

## America the Beautiful

America, America, you've brought many things
from donuts and pizza to new songs my kids sing

No longer the Chinese anthem in a red scarved sea,
but, "Don't Cha Wish your Girlfriend was Hot like Me."

Wal-Mart and Redbox for movies and treats.
Finding the toilet instead of peeing on streets.

Running and jumping barefoot and outside.
Kids streaking the lawn with glory and pride.

Ordering pepperoni pizza and fries like a waffle,
no pig ears, duck blood or things I deem awful.

Chips with salsa and cheese til I ache.
"But I won't eat this in China!" is the excuse that I'll take.

Car rides with heat and a radio inside,
to drive and to shuttle and sometimes just hide.

With all of the fun and all of the joys;
it's time for us to head to the motherland of noise.

It's time to eat veggies and wash our feet;
from the grime and the stories our legs will soon meet.

God has a journey for our family to learn
how to have hearts that will long and yearn

to depend on Him and listen for His voice;
treading the unfamiliar, but given a choice.

Seek out the Lord until He answers my pleas
fight for joy and fight on my knees.

He is reminding me daily of our calling and love
for Him and the people living below and above.

### still not home

Our kids are feeling more and more ready to head home each day. Sage, my animated nine-year old keeps telling me that she wants to go back to China because America is nice, but it's way too organized. And it has tons of rules.

She tells me "I mean, ugh, if you want to buy something, you have to like, go into a store. You can't just get stuff on the streets like in China. And, the traffic takes forever! What is it with Americans stopping at all the red lights?!?"

On a roll, she continues on her oh-so-genetically-pre-dispositioned rant. "And all the rules. In China, you just do whatever you want. I mean, you can pee wherever, listen to music wherever. It's just more relaxed and free."

She's right. For her, seeing little boys urinate in trashcans and street vendors selling ducks with their heads still attached is home. She misses it. And you know, I'm beginning to miss it too.

It's funny how we just can't exempt ourselves from the cliché "the grass is always greener." It seems that while I'm in China, America can do no wrong. Then when I'm in America, I crave all things Chinese. It's also why women never like their own hair. We want what we can't have. What is it with us human beings?! It's because Jesus is the only thing that satisfies. If I could just staple that to my forehead, maybe I would actually begin living like He does.

### finding God in the wait

As I hear stories of friends I miss in China, I sit here and wait. We have been waiting for medical clearance for five months now. Historically, I have not waited well. But this time around, I don't want to wait like a bratty child who sits with their arms folded at the dinner table waiting for their mothers to serve them dessert instead of dinner. I want to sit in awe and gratefulness that He has given me another day to serve Him. But gratefulness in the wait is as hard to find as good Chinese food in America.

I sat in the car as I waited for my kids this afternoon and the Lord spoke clearly to me about His wisdom in our wait. Here we go.

*Proverbs 2:1-5 (ESV)*

*"My son, if you receive my words*
*and treasure up my commandments with you,*

*making your ear attentive to wisdom*
*and inclining your heart to understanding;*

*yes, if you call out for insight*
*and raise your voice for*
*understanding,*

*if you seek it like silver*
*and search for it as for hidden*
*treasures,*

*then you will understand the fear of*
*the Lord*
*and find the knowledge of God."*

This proverb is chalk full of insights into the heart of God, but I'm only going to touch on a few. There are several things in these Scriptures that walk us through understanding God, not just knowing Him. There is an if/then clause, which means you have to work backwards a little. The hope is that in the end, we "will understand the fear of the Lord and find the knowledge of God." (Prov. 2:5) So, in knowing the result we obviously need to understand the path to get there. Start back up at Proverbs 2:1:

In order to know the Lord in my wait, I have to:

1. Receive
   Receiving the Lord's words means humility for us. In order to receive, you must empty your hands. If your hands are already full, you will be incapable of handling anything the Lord wants to give you. My desire to be right is what normally takes up space in my hands. I have to put that down so that I can receive more from God.

2. Treasure His commandments
   Treasuring His commandments means we have to protect ourselves in the Word. We only treasure things we value and want to show off to other people, like newborn pictures or a sparkling engagement ring. His commandments are a means of sanctifying us and glorifying Himself. They aren't

oppressive and legalistic; rather, they point us to our need for Jesus, and that is something to be treasured and shared.

3. Make my ear attentive

When I am trying to watch a movie or hear lyrics to a song, I need an attentive ear. For me that means that all talking, tapping pencils, and scraping of chairs has to cease. I am diligent about making it quiet because I want to hear whatever it is that I am listening to. Do I work that hard to hear God? Do I make space and time for stillness? Bottom line is that when a good movie wants my ear's attention, I make it happen. I pray that I am that intentional in my times with the Lord. There is a reason that God created coffee and I believe that getting my tired body out of bed in the morning to commune with Him is the main one.

4. Incline my heart

When we incline our hearts towards something, we lean into it. We press in. And honestly, when we lean into the Lord, it means that we are leaning away from other things and other people. I have to ask myself, am I leaning so far into a worldly ambition or identity that if it gets pulled out from under me, I fall?

5. Call out for insight

There are several times that we find ourselves calling out. We raise our voices because we feel angry, excited, or that we aren't being heard. All three of these can be summarized by saying that we are desperate, and we feel that just speaking would be an insufficient expression of our hearts. When we are calling out, we are expressing our deep desperation for God to respond in some way.

6. We seek out the Lord's wisdom like silver and search for it as for hidden treasure.

If I knew that silver was hidden for me to have if I could just find it, I would be consistent and relentless in my pursuit. The time spent searching wouldn't be a burden nor would it cause anxiety because I know that the reward is good. I wait and search patiently because I know that what I get in the end is both present and valuable.

This is where I find myself now. We don't know if and when we will head back to China. There is no guarantee for us in any of the blood testing that is happening for our daughter. But if I grow anxious in my waiting for answers, then when I finally have them, my response will be "Well, it's about time God! I've been waiting a LONG time. Finally!" But if my wait is patient, hopeful and full of trusting in verses like Proverbs 2, then my wait will be blanketed in thankfulness and hope. Whenever God finds it good to share His plans with us, I will be grateful and humbled instead of acting like a spoiled kid at dinnertime.

I find comfort in the fact that God took a long time to save Paul. You see, God saw Saul persecuting His church. He saw the pain that Saul was causing, the destructive path he was leaving behind him. God saw all this and yet waited for Paul's conversion. God had the bigger picture in sight. God apparently saw that if He waited then He would get more glory.

The summary of what I have learned as we wait is that God doesn't owe it to me to tell me the when, how, where and why of our wait. As a matter of fact, I'm not sure the end result is the part that God is ultimately concerned with. He is concerned with how we wait. It's in that tension that we grow. It is at that point of limbo that we call out in desperation and seek a God who is bigger than us. God knows this about humans, so He lets us wait because He knows that we will come out in the end with a deeper love and satisfaction in having Him as our Rescuer.

Wait graciously. God wants our waiting. Let Him rest on your hearts and grant you peace beyond all understanding because He is a good, loving and sovereign God.

# Transition and Moist: Two Words I Hate

"Accept that some days you are the pigeon,
and some days you are the statue."

David Brent

*Now that the medicals are done, books are bought, and fajitas sufficiently eaten our lives would begin to transition. We would start the long process of saying good-bye and packing up a family of seven to move back home to China.*

### saying goodbye

My best friend and I spent the morning wrestling with my kids and eating a picnic in the 75-degree Texas winter. I cleared the plates slowly and pretended to fold the blanket over and over again, avoiding the thing that I had grown to hate: good-byes. You would think that I would get better at this. She asked me if I was hungry and I commented that I could feel the pit in my stomach growing, but it wasn't hunger. I knew it was coming. The inevitable part of my day where I would say good-bye to someone that I loved dearly. She and I both knew that it would be 3-4 years until I saw her again. My daughter would be a teenager by that point. She could have babies that I would never get to see until they chewing gum and scribbling letters on bathroom walls. Dreams would be achieved, disappointments will settle in, arguments would be had, and reconciliation would happen. I would be there for none of it.

My kids would miss the grandparents taking them for ice cream and handing them a dollar to buy jawbreakers larger than their mouths can handle. Their friends would have birthday parties, slumber parties and memories, none of which my children would be a part of. All of these things we would miss in each other's lives. All of those realities balled themselves up and started kickboxing me in the stomach.

I got very emotional about the whole thing. The reality of being deleted from people's lives for a season is painful. More painful than I liked to admit. I cried for the entire morning. I would see her say good-bye to my four-year old son and I would have to pretend to take out the trash so that I wouldn't loose it. I would hear her talk about her plans for this summer and I would have to saunter around and clear the picnic (again), putting the meager scraps into a plastic bag. All of the sudden there was no trash left, so I picked microscopic pieces of grass off the blanket and when that was accomplished, I could only cry.

I hate crying in public because I am not a cute crier. I look like a cat ambushed me and mauled my face. I cannot fake my crying because there are huge streaks of red running from my eyelids to my chin. It's lovely and doesn't allow me to lie and blame it on an infected tear duct.

When you live overseas, it's deeply painful to miss out on the lives of family and friends. Oftentimes, your instinct is to put up walls. Every fiber of your being wants to disconnect, pretend to move on and settle in. And then one day you read a blog or you see a picture that reminds you of all the things you aren't experiencing with the people you love. At that point, your walls and defenses are either strengthened or crumbled. Missing out is a powerful force that makes us do weird things. Sometimes it will make you really resent your calling and question living so far away. It might even make you justify an early return stateside. At that point, all there is to do is to plead with Jesus to turn those emotions into affections and not resentments. My prayer is usually along the lines of Psalm 90:14 "Satisfy us in the morning with your steadfast love; so that I may rejoice and be glad all our days." Jesus has to be the satisfaction that bears the weight of my not being among people with whom I have so much history.

I wonder if in a way, it was easier for expats (people who are living outside the bounds of their home country) who lived a hundred years ago. The modern conveniences were absent but so was the Internet that acted as a reminder that you had people who care for you living an ocean away. There was no email or Facebook to help keep you partially connected to your friends and unfortunately disconnected from the new culture you were living in.

When culture stress is hard, I find myself clinging to emails. It is a simple reminder that sits in my inbox that I am not forgotten. For a long time, I tried to deny that I missed people in America. I told myself that I had moved on and that China would be my home in every regard. And for the most part, it is. But there is something about relationships that have history, people who knew you when you crimped your bangs or held your children hours after they were born. Those relationships that lovingly tell you there is spinach in your teeth and bitterness in your heart.

When you set a date to head back overseas, people make all kinds of promises. They vow to email every week, to send packages and to sit down with their husbands to discuss a trip to visit. While all of these are well intended, we have learned to not hope in most of them. Because after awhile, jobs get busy, kids have dance recitals and budgets get cut. If we hope in any of these promises, we will be left with anger and frustration all while our friends simply remember that they had good intentions.

My goal for this time around was to cherish those friendships. I didn't want to deny their power and presence in my life. They are important to me and help me to love Jesus. Allowing them to speak into my life helps me to have the ability to walk out my door in China to face a sea of strangers. If you have friends that live overseas, here are a few things that you can do to tell them you love them:

> Send email. Even if it's something trivial, like, "I ran into your grandmother at the Bingo hall last night. She won a $15 dollar gift certificate to Luby's and a meatloaf." Send them that email. They will smile and then feel like they are connected to your world in some small way.

> Send care packages. Pack them with the small things that mean a lot to your friend. It doesn't have to be big, just meaningful. Ask them what things they are craving and put those in. If you can't afford a care package, maybe send an e-card or buy them a single song online and send it their way.

> Pray for them. And then tell them that you are praying for them. Your friend wants to be reminded that there are people in the States contending for them and their work.

> Go see them. I realize this is rather impractical for most people. But if you have the resources and

can get time off then do it. I cannot tell you how refreshing it is to have friends come and see your world. You would experience the sounds and smells that make up your friend's home and hopefully get a glimpse of what the world looks like outside of comfort.

Ask them questions about what their days are like. Don't assume your friend is too busy to answer your curiosities. It shows them that you want to understand their day. We've had lots of people tell us that they were afraid to email us because of security. If you are talking about your personal life and what is going on, there is no problem in most places. Ask your friend for email parameters.

We have even had families that get their kids to send our kids emails. This engages our children and gives American kids a glimpse into life overseas.

Be creative and be consistent. This will speak volumes and will sustain that person when days get discouraging and they want to use the words in their new language that they learned on the street, but shouldn't repeat to anybody.

### how i know it's time to go home

We finally have tickets to head home to China. I've discovered over the past week or so several indications that it is indeed time for us to return to China.

I've been biting my cuticles again. Not my nails, but my cuticles. When you bite your nails, you also risk tasting crusty food from lunch. And the taste lingers until you find that brownie from last night. Brownies solve most medical or emotional emergencies. Especially when you make the brownies with applesauce instead of oil because that way you can eat 4 times as many. My Chinese friends would rather lick the bottom of a trashcan at CiCi's Pizza than stick their fingers in their mouths. So we've adapted this habit too. Well, I did until I lived in the land of freedom and cleanliness for 8 months.

It doesn't feel strange to walk around the house with the same shoes you wore outside. In China, the second you walk in a home you remove your shoes and put on slippers. If you've ever lived in Asia, you would adopt this habit about 7 minutes after leaving the airport terminal. You basically walk on urine, feces, tofu, lottery tickets and plastic bags until they have assimilated themselves into the pavement. I won't go 12 inches in my house without taking my shoes off in China. I did that in America for about 6 months and then I noticed myself wearing my shoes inside the house.

Cheese and meat don't cause my colon to rise up and call me traitor. When we first landed in the States, the introduction of dairy and servings of meat the size of my thighbone made my stomach really ache. Fast-forward through many meals involving queso and pork ribs, and I seem to be cured of my stomach's rebellion to American food.

The final and possibly most compelling reason we need to get back to China on the quick is that this week I have heard both Sage and my seven-year old son Corbin singing, "Don't Cha Wish Your Girlfriend was Hot like Me?"

### A Poem about Packing

About 4 weeks until we fly
things to do I can only describe

Packing and cleaning for a family of 7
makes me yearn, aching for life in heaven

There are 14 check-ins and as many to carry
lots of coffee or this could get scary.

Movie screens on the seats are my new best friend
six movies later, my kids' trip will end.

Heading towards security makes me shiver
and gives TSA an ulcer on their liver.

People run and people hide
when they see us coming to their side
of the line that winds to and fro
I hear them praying we aren't in their row.

If we make it to China with computers and kids
a victory dance happens and we take a bid
which parent will fall first, asleep in the night
not waking 'til we see the bright morning light.

Now back to the packing, I cannot delay
from a month to a week and then finally one day.

## what not to say to moms

When people discover the actual date you are leaving the country again, panic sets in. We have been in the States for eight months, but it's the last few weeks that guilt people into seeing us just one last time. We love these people and we laugh every time it happens. But there are also those people who like the idea of getting together, but in the end their schedules demand of them other things. As a stay-at-home mother of five, I've learned to remember that most people schedule their days in pencil for a reason.

There are a few things that I'm going to share with you that will save you a lot of heartache. If you are a friend or family member of a mom that has lots of small kids at home, I have a brief list of things NOT to do.

1.  Do not plan a girl's night, retreat, double date, or long lunch without kids, only to cancel the plans last minute. Why? Because chances are the mom in question has been looking forward to that time all week. And an even better chance that it's that very event that has kept her from going postal on several occasions. The mother will be gracious about you canceling, but then will retreat to the bathroom and cry for five minutes. She will have to blame her pollen allergies when her kids ask her what is wrong.

2.  Do not ask her why her kids are not walking, talking, rolling over, potty trained, or sleeping in their own beds yet. This will cause a snowball of thoughts that will end in all of her kids being homeless or in jail.

3.  Do not ask her to make a dessert last minute for a function that she is attending outside her own home. She will say yes, of course, because saying no would imply that she does not have everything together and she is afraid she will be de-frocked from the Super Moms club. Also, that mom will feel guilty if she uses a five minute boxed dessert because others will know. They just will. So she will go to the store, because there is always one ingredient that is missing. The domino effects of this dessert request will send her into panic mode...quickly.

4.  Do not complain about how tired and busy you are because you have to go to the gym and then meet at Starbucks today. This will cause her to sin.

5.  Do not talk about how you never see the sun rise because you get up after 8 every morning. And how on the weekends you sleep in until 10 and then eat a late breakfast just in time for kick-off at 11. She will be tempted to start "accidently" calling you at 4:30 from her husband's phone (so you don't recognize the number, of course) and then hang up quickly. Then she will fall peacefully back to sleep feeling oh so pleased with herself.

Actions like the ones above will send your friend into Mommy Depression. You don't want to see Mommy Depression. It's not pretty.

This has been a Public Service Announcement from me. You're welcome.

### hopping the pond

Our luggage consists of 14 check-ins, 16 carry-ons. When you have five children and a pile of carry-ons, you throw security into convulsions and they forget to check how many things you are actually carrying on. They also weigh about 75 pounds each because they never check that either. After a brief 48 hours of traveling, we found home. When you travel with a large family, you kind of just hold your breath until you find a bed to sleep in for more than one night at a time. The gift God has sent to parents is the creation of adrenaline and on-demand movie screens. Adrenaline was created to keep traveling families and stay-at-home mothers out of jail.

On demand movie screens were definitely engineered by a mother traveling with five children. Our older three kids sit together in one row and we tell them to stay on the kid's channel, don't order caffeine, and we'll see you in Beijing. My husband takes one little one and I take the other one. We've got the whole system down to a science, including but not limited to throwing security our most pathetic faces so that they let us enter the diplomatic security line.

We have been really nervous about our language since we were gone for almost 8 months. There were moments that I pictured myself trying to buy watermelon and instead asking some fruit vendor to be the father of my children. Nothing that dramatic has happened…but there's still time. It's only been three days since arriving back home in China and my body is running out of adrenaline to pump through my exhausted veins. I'm sure things will get interesting here pretty soon.

Because we are white, have five kids (one of them being black), are American, push a double stroller and speak Chinese, we are like a walking three-ring circus. Imagine seeing a family in the States that has 21 kids and all of them are blue. You would stare, take not-so-subtle pictures with your cell phone, nudge your mother to look, and come up to ask all types of questions. That's our life. We have been here for three days and have already had numerous pictures taken, been followed, eaten lunch with 30 onlookers, had our hair touched, and been told that we shouldn't be able to speak Chinese because we are American. The funny thing is that even though there are a million things that define us as foreigners, the longer we've lived here, the more it feels like home. When we arrived a few days ago, our entire family commented that we felt content and comfortable, and this was despite the fact that we had moved to a new city upon arrival.

Our time in America was fabulous. The time was spent huddling into the lives of the people we love. But, we weren't home. It is similar to flipping a pancake too early. There is always some batter left on the pan and the pancake is left with holes and pieces missing. Visiting the States is fun but filled with holes for us and we never quite feel at home while living there. The chaos in China makes sense to us. We have never lived in this new city before, but it's as though our hearts have been prepared. Our lives have been readied to live and to love.

## my first attempt at speaking chinese

When we first moved to China, we were located up near the frozen tundra bordering Siberia. Harbin is home to one of the largest ice festivals in the world. While being stuck walking through the Taj Mahal made completely of ice, go-go dancers shimmying, Indian music blaring, pushing your 15-month-old daughter wearing 4 pairs of socks over her hands might seem glorious, it's also really, really cold. Being cold is one of my personal hells. My personal hell also involves me eating spam straight out of the can. Now that we can claim we've done the ice festival, we don't have to ever do it again. Ever.

When we touched down in China for the first time, my eyes took notice of every moving shadow and wrinkled forehead that passed through my peripherals. Even just walking through the airport terminal for the first time causes your head to sway back and forth trying to make sense of everything at once. The bus hired to bring us to the university where we would live zipped around traffic like pigeons flocking for bread. Everyone seemed to be attacking the road and assaulting each other as if the last morsel in existence had just been dropped to the ground. As we approached our new home, I couldn't help but notice that our building was nested between two coal factories. The smoke had been billowing up creating a welcoming banner of gray. We climbed the stairs in our apartment building and opened the door to our new lives. Our apartment was on the fifth floor of a building rusted from the five long years it had housed occupants. The layout went like this: concrete, concrete, concrete, door, concrete, drain for the shower, washer and toilet, concrete. The sharp, harsh corners of each room defined my heart's discontent I was feeling as I left America. The layers of coal on my floor that I peeled away each day acted as a reminder that comfort was going to be an illusive mirage I could only hope to grasp.

It was week three and my body still required a solid nine hours of sleep every night, partnered with an hour-long nap each afternoon. The stimulation of my surroundings had taken its toll on my body. One day, as I laid down on my bed and watched the smoke stacks puff their cancerous rings into the sky, I heard something that startled me from my half conscious state. A dog was yelping, followed by deep hoarse laughter. I looked down and watched in horror as two coal factory workers took turns torturing this scrappy white dog. I bent down on all fours onto my bed and started to cry. It was another cultural rock that had been thrown into my dry riverbed of understanding.

I could only say 'hello' in Chinese at that point and I'm not sure it would have been helpful to yell a friendly greeting out the window. So I picked up a phrase book and found something that I could pronounce. I said it a few times over and over again to myself until I had it memorized. I hiked myself up onto the windowsill and cleared my throat. They were still beating the dog and watching this empowered me to shout my phrase out the window. "Stop it bastard!" came rolling off my tongue in broken Chinese.

The men looked up in amazement at the words they just heard coming out of some white woman's mouth. They chuckled to themselves and the dog withdrew behind the safety of an abandoned tire. I was crying and frantic, but I felt good that at least the torturing had stopped. Unfortunately, that entire episode has forever seared that Chinese phrase into my head. When the bird lady that lived downstairs told me that I was fat and a horrible parent for the 15th time in a day, that phrase crawled down from the archives and almost made its way to the lady's ears. And the person who shoved my luggage aside while they catapulted themselves into my taxi just might have heard the phrase. I'm not proud of this, but I did end up in the taxi.

Our first few months of living here were rough. I found myself running for comfort to the inbox of our email and setting up Skype dates with friends every other day. Not only were we living in a strange country, but I was now at home with Sage, my 15-month old daughter all day…for the first time. The 'me' that had clear definitions in the States was now being tossed aside in order for someone completely new to take up residence in my shell of a person.

### Ode to "Convenient Noodles" (the Ramen Noodle counterpart in China)

When we got back to China we had no home. We would throw the luggage and ourselves into a friend's apartment for the night and tackle apartment hunting in the morning. Because we had no bowls, stove, or kitchen we resorted to eating convenient noodles twice a day for about two weeks.

"Convenient Noodles" how I loathe you so
In my colon you stop the flow

Pre-packaged noodles hard as a rock
Tiny processed packets of chicken stock

Dehydrated veggies to add to my soup
I'd only choose to eat these if I had croup.

But these last few days of moving and stress
I love you more and loathe you less.

6 quick minutes and my family can eat
Feeding 7 people for only two-ninety three.

Without a kitchen and without a home
I will not complain, I will not groan

At the everyday occurrence of you at our table
Fast and easy, you are true to your label.

"Convenient Noodles" I love you so
No matter my colon, no matter the flow.

## not being indirect

When I moved to China, one of many of my misplaced expectations was that the Chinese were indirect. I guess I always envisioned women passing quietly by like a quiet breeze, most of the time going unnoticed until the air became still. But I have found that most Chinese are like a tropical storm, brewing and stirring until they finally touch land. There will be destruction and turmoil in their wake, but as far as they are concerned, they are casually blowing by, removing unwanted debris. Most Chinese are slow to speak, but that doesn't mean they are quiet. Their words can be both direct and forceful.

While the Chinese are indirect in some ways (mostly regarding confrontation or instructions), they can be very direct in most other ways. We had an American friend who was teaching her English class on the first day. She was one of those ladies that has more of a pear shaped body, so she is smaller on the top and a little bigger on the bottom. As she finished up the class, she walked away from the podium and went out into the classroom to chat with the students. Immediately, two female students went up to her and told her that they thought she was a beautiful teacher...UNTIL she stepped out from behind the podium and they saw that she was heavier on the bottom. They boldly told this to her face. After giving birth to my fourth child, a day didn't go by that someone didn't come up to me and ask me what I had been eating because I was really fat. I lost my baby weight and people started telling me that I was looking too skinny.

Two American friends of ours were riding in a taxi in Beijing one day when the driver suddenly pulled over. He saw the approaching hill and told them that they were too fat and that his taxi would surely not make it up the hill with both of them in the backseat. He made one of them get out and find another ride.

On a weekly basis, a stranger in an elevator or random taxi driver will ask us how much money we make or what we pay in rent. Women have approached me to tell me that I look tired and have too many wrinkles. Strangers in the market have pointed to my children and explained to me which one is the prettiest or the smartest of the five. Most of the time, I can understand culturally what they are trying to do: they are assessing where to place us in terms of society. They are estimating our value in the community. When they remark about being fat or skinny or not eating right, they are trying to take care of me. If I am too fat, then they want to see me start exercising so that I can live a long, peaceful life. If my body is looking ragged, I need to eat more vegetables so that I have energy to take care of my children.

While pretty much all of these questions are social suicide in America, they are commonplace and loving here. I have tried to see them that way, and for the most part I do now. When we first moved here though, I would find myself weeping quietly in the bathroom after being told for the fifth time that I was looking fat. One day, I was told by a lady that I looked fat and another lady that I looked too skinny. At this point, I threw the proverbial white flag at trying to please anybody.

And because criticizing younger people is a way for the older generation to love and care for them, it really doesn't matter how hard I try because there will always be something new for them to tell me to fix.

## what i am not guaranteed

I am not guaranteed tomorrow.
I am not guaranteed that my children will be safe.

I am not guaranteed that sickness won't begin to ravage my body…starting right now.

I am not guaranteed our financial safety won't get cut away.

I am not guaranteed that people will like me.

But…

I am promised that He will never leave me nor forsake me.

I am promised that in the end, Jesus will get the victory.

I am promised love, joy, peace, patience, kindness, goodness, faithfulness, gentleness and self-control.

I am promised that tomorrow morning new mercies will be waiting for me at my bedside.

I am promised only this one moment. And with that one moment I can choose to be fearful of what I am not guaranteed or roll around in the freedom of the promises that are already mine.

# Letting the Dust Settle

"A bird does not sing because it has an answer.
It sings because it has a song."

Chinese Proverb

*It's nice to be home. Our furniture arrived on the moving truck at midnight wherein we gave our friends an opportunity to earn treasures in heaven by lugging our stuff up three flights of stairs at two in the morning. We found an apartment and have finished the task of cleaning out the dust and memories of the former tenants.*

## finding roots

I spent an hour or so yesterday walking around our new apartment complex taking pictures and breathing in our new surroundings.

Home only feels like home to me when I have a sense for what surrounds me aesthetically. I want to understand which trees are so satisfied as to plant deep roots; which trees provide shade for afternoon discussions between husbands and wives; to walk past the magnolia trees that bloom into smiles from back windows. I want to discover the tree that seems to keep watch over us while confidently grounding its presence among much more glorious counterparts. I want to look up and find the most optimistic of trees planted in unlikely places. To walk under the canopy of palms that promises fresh mangoes and short winters. To happen upon old roots dug up to remind us that death of one brings life to another. To breathe in stalky bamboos whistling their hellos.

It's all part of settling in. I guess we all just want to know we understand and are understood. Our lives have just begun in this new place but peace has been found and that is home enough for me.

## amelia bedelia

We have finally settled in and set up house in our new city. When you move into an apartment here, whatever is in the apartment is your issue. We have spent hours cleaning kitchens and throwing away broken chairs that belonged to the previous tenants. When the trash lady came to carry away some big items, I asked her if she had a friend that would like to be our house helper. Five minutes later a woman was on my couch being interviewed. That was it. She would now be an important part of our family's life in this new city.

Do you remember that endearing children's character Amelia Bedelia? She is a house helper for a wealthy Rogers family. She makes all kinds of mistakes like when Mrs. Rogers tells her to draw the curtains so that the furniture won't fade, Amelia pulls out a pencil and a sketch pad to start drawing. She makes all kinds of blunders like this. She always ends up baking a pie to pacify the anger of the Rogers when they return home and see the disaster of a job she has done.

First of all, I struggled with the idea of having a house helper for a long time. I felt like I owned a slave. It was uncomfortable to me and, honestly, I prided myself on having a gaggle of children and not needing any help. Life over here just takes a long time. You can only shop one or two days at a time. In order to buy meat, fruit, vegetables, and spices, you sometimes need to visit two or three different markets and stores. Everything is done on foot, and you carry those heavy bags with you to each new place. There is no picking up a frozen lasagna and popping it in the oven for an hour. All meals are made from scratch.

My friends eventually convinced me that I had lost it and needed to suck it up and get some help. In that same life season, I was outside one day with my kids, talking to some older women. When I told people that I didn't need a house helper, I felt pride rising up. I swear I could hear drummer boys beating out "Glory, Glory Hallelujah." I just knew that I had reached the pinnacle of super woman by managing my home overseas with absolutely no outside help. As I awaited the praise that I was sure was about to be spoken, I instead heard, "You don't have a house helper?? How can you be a good mom to all those children?" When these women heard that I didn't have a house helper, they immediately saw a neglectful mother. It was a good cultural lesson that eventually also turned into a repentant heart. Funny how often those two are tied for me.

That brings me to now. Our sweet house helper has been with us for two months and it's become quite humorous to me as we dance around trying to get used to each other's footing. There's been some clumsy two stepping, but we're getting better and better. She's from the village, so her education level is very low. This past week, Osama Bin Laden was killed and we were talking with her and a friend about it at lunch. She had never heard of Osama Bin Laden or 9/11. We tried explaining what happened at 9/11 and she just stared at us blankly. We stopped the conversation quickly because we didn't want her to lose any more face than she already had lost by not having a clue as to what we were describing.

A week or so ago I asked her to pick up some vanilla ice cream from the store. She came home with Taro root. Which is just like vanilla ice cream except for, well…the vanilla. Both were in ice cream form, but drastically differed in color and taste. She had no idea how to read the characters for vanilla, so she just guessed. Again, the loss of face would be too much to just admit not knowing how to read.

Just yesterday, I had made some homemade BBQ sauce. If you've ever made something that requires more ingredients than an egg, water, and a box of something, then you know it's hard to make things from scratch. I had made a huge batch of BBQ sauce and needed it stored for the evening. She took the sauce and put it in a peanut butter jar. That jar was still half filled with peanut butter. Speaking of peanut butter, she consistently takes our used peanut butter jars out of the trash to bring them home to use as storage containers. I love her resourcefulness. I often find her sewing together our broken plastic sandals or taking a half-eaten peach out of the trash in order to not be wasteful. She lives in one room with her husband. Not a one-bedroom apartment, but one room total. The heat index yesterday was 107, and she has no air conditioner or kitchen.

At first, I was frustrated by these things that seemed so obvious to me. But then I realized that she was raised in a totally different world than I've ever known. She grew up in a China that had her eating bark as a child because of the lack of resources available at that time. As a young girl, she couldn't waste her time on learning all the characters needed to be literate. In order to obtain literacy here, you have to be very diligent in learning characters. It is straight memorization. In contrast to the alphabet, where my three-year old can learn to read, Chinese kids are dependent on adults and teachers to read to them until they have memorized a few hundred characters. There is no real sounding out that a child can do, they either know the character or they don't. And the tricky thing is that the characters can have only a tiny stroke of difference, so it is very easy to get them mixed up. This is a mountainous task to undertake. Our house helper just didn't have the time or ability to learn what she needed to be able to read as an adult. All she could do was focus on survival. She then went on to tell me that her father became terminally ill when she was 12, so she dropped out of school for a year to take care of him.

Because of this background, she saves everything. Almost daily, I see her foraging through our trashcan for bottles, jars, cans, and boxes. She takes them all home and either sells them or uses them for storage. This morning she was drinking her water out of one of our spicy pepper jars that I had thrown away. We have had several Amelia Bedelia moments. Just like Mrs. Rogers, I'm learning to be more explicit with my instructions by explaining what I need instead of expecting her to read instructions and by embracing her resourcefulness. She cooks with no lights on in the kitchen and only uses electricity when absolutely necessary. I've grown quite attached to her and it seems as if she's getting used to me too.

### the day we almost got mauled by a wolf

This was the first time in our life in China that there has been a swimming pool in our apartment complex. The excitement about this little fact started at 6:30 a.m. the days we decided to go swimming. On one of our first times to head out to the pool, we ran into an unexpected visitor.

My five little sheep and I almost got mauled by a wolf.

Why, you might ask, does a wolf live in a city of 6 million people? With a straight face I will tell you, "Never, ever ask why. That is a dangerous question when living overseas. Just keep it to yourself and keep smiling."

Summer is in full swing and swimming is one of the only sane things to do with five kids. I slathered on sunscreen and we tore off to meet friends at the pool mid-morning. The double stroller was weighed down with all things inflatable. We looked like a walking trade show. One child was crammed in the front seat with his head lodged under a floatie. An old lady across the street yelled at me. She was vigilantly told me that there was NO way all those children were mine. After I affirmed this a good eight times, she decided I was lying and scooted across the street to further interrogate my children. As we were having this friendly little discussion, my peripherals noticed a stirring in the bushes. The very large dog-like creature had been resting under the shade of a tree when his curiosity got the best of him. He decided to come our way. As he stumbled up to where we were, I noticed that this indeed was not a nice domesticated animal, but a mangy, rabies-infested wolf. His eyes had crusty white circles around them and his mouth was dripping with foam. His fur was dark brown and was twisted into dreadlocks covering the patches of scars and disease. Dreds are fine on nomadic Bob Marley fans that travel the country selling hemp ankle bracelets out of their trunk, but on a sick dog, there is much need for concern.

Normally, when I see a stray dog, I make a game plan on how best to drop-kick it to Northern Mongolia. Had I tried to drop kick this thing, it would have taken off my leg. At this point, the old lady who was grilling me about my family was now screaming and running around like a bee had flown up her shorts. She wailed in fear for a security guard while another man called the police. The wolf had now sauntered over to my area. I grabbed all of my kids and threw them behind the bushes. I told them to face the wall and not talk. Sage was crying, Joi's face was jammed into the concrete, and Corbin was not within arm's reach. I used the stroller to barricade us in and frantically grabbed Corbin to my side.

Earlier, I had been upset with myself for forgetting to bring snacks. Snacks are always an important pool outing element because they give me a reason for a fake safety break so that I can get warm. Mr. Wolf is now sniffing in our stroller looking for food. Thank you Jesus that I'm so disorganized. There was no food to be found. At that point I was having a Jack Bauer complex, and I found my mind figuring out ways to cram the stroller into his jugular. Quickly reminding myself that I was in fact NOT Jack Bauer, I forced myself to take a more passive stance.

After circling in our area for a few minutes, he galloped over to the old lady. She had dropped her bag of groceries and he was tearing into it. Now old lady was not just scared, she was ticked. If there is one thing you need to know about Chinese grandmothers, it's that buying groceries is no laughing matter. They take it very seriously and now big wolf dude was eating her fish, meat, and plastic bags. She began crying, stomping her legs and yelling at the wolf to stop eating her dumplings.

As he started in on her bag, I saw an opportunity to get my kids out of there. I whispered to them, "RUN, RUN, RUN." There was a fence about fifty feet away, and I knew that if we could reach it we would be safe. Albeit for a much less valiant cause, I did feel a bit like Harriet Tubman smuggling slaves behind the cloak of night. I was pushing the stroller in one hand and had a child dangling in my other hand, running towards the fence. Once we finally reached the safety zone, we felt relief as if we'd just crossed the border into a freed man's territory.

The kids and I were all visibly shaking. By that point, about ten security guards had come and were trying to solve the little wolf issue. But not even policemen carry guns here, so I'm not sure what they were going to do with the thing. All I know is that we were all safe.

*loving jesus terribly*

I am sitting in a quiet house, eating leftover spaghetti with spicy pepper sauce and a cold Coke Zero. My generous and wonderful friend, DY, took the kids for a sleepover. All of them. At the same time.

I'm actually not sure what I'm going to write at the moment. My wonderfully disciplined husband would never start writing with no idea of how it's going to end. But that's just who I am. As with most things, I start enthusiastically and hope that in the process nobody gets maimed or loses a limb.

Here's the deal: I am not at all like Jesus.

Do I want to be? Yes, desperately. Am I even close? No. For instance, I just dropped a chopstick on the floor and left it there. I looked for it for a brief second, couldn't find it immediately and then took a small lick of the sauce from off the floor. Jesus would not have done that. He would have persevered and found the chopstick. I'm not sure about licking sauce from off the floor. It's a great sauce so I'm pretty sure he might have licked it.

Lately I have realized that I can't love people well who are different than me. And honestly, I get annoyed by too many people. Food smackers, line cutters, spitters, ABC appliqué jumpsuit wearing elementary school teachers, Christian singers who don't sing about God...ever, cute camp girls, people who say 'just' 62 times while they are praying, and the list goes on really. They all annoyingly grab at me like a dripping shower curtain clinging to my legs. That's ridiculous. Jesus wouldn't think like that either.

I still want to look cute and sassy. I feel like I shouldn't still breakout on my 35-year old face, but I do. And it bothers me. I want to get cute haircuts that sashay in the breeze, wear cute scarves that match the changing leaves of fall, and to wear cute winter boots with those little dangling tassels. I shouldn't care. But I do. Jesus wouldn't do that. He's never consumed with fitting in. Yet, so often my mind calculates what to say, how to dress, when to laugh, what to read, all based on what the world tells me I should do in order to have people flock to my side.

My life is covered in failings, but it is also spotted in grace. Praise the Lord for Jesus and His example, and that God gave us the cross and the Holy Spirit so that we have the ability to change our affections. You can't muster up affections. They are gifted to us. I pray on a daily basis that my affections would be for Christ and His character.

## Chinese exercising

I love the way people here exercise. I've loved it since day one. These are the activities I saw by just looking out my kitchen window in our new apartment this morning:

1. A man and a woman ballroom dancing.

2. A woman twirling a racquet around while she spins and tries to keep the ball lying in the center from falling. Most of the time this little balancing dance routine is done with 20 others. It's fantastic to watch them all balance this ball around and twirl around like little girls in their new Easter dresses.

3. A man with his shirt off and hands raised as if he is being accosted by the police. He is walking backwards with his arms raised, waving side to side and chanting a mantra.

4. A man with a long pole doing kung fu moves. Similar to Kung Fu Panda...well, except for the panda. I didn't see any pandas at our apartment complex today. Bummer, that would've been great.

5. A woman beating her chest and abdomen as she walks.

6. A woman beating her fingers against the wall. They like to beat themselves in order to get the blood flowing. Not many days go by that I don't see people banging their backs against a tree or smacking their legs into a lamppost.

7. A group doing Tai Chi. This is a VERY slow dance that looks a little like yoga, except that yoga probably burns calories. We laugh at how slow Tai Chi can be. I've done it and it's relaxing, but not as easy as it looks. It's meant to remove stress, heal your body and help you take a more defensive posture if attacked. But I will say that with Tai Chi, you are moving so slow that if somebody came by, stole your purse and gave you a swift kick in the shin, tai chi moves aren't going to help.

8.    Ladies dancing with red, feathery fans.
9.    Men fighting the air with wooden swords.
10.   A man with a long javelin spinning around in circles.

All of this happens each morning. And most of these activities are done while still wearing pajamas. I love it. Sometimes in the evening, couples young and old will be on a stroll by the river in their matching pajamas. It sounds like a theater of Eastern chaos, but it's actually really fun to watch. I so admire the older generation here because they are outside everyday exercising and keeping their minds active. It's a joy to watch, and I'm hoping to learn a thing or two about relieving stress by observing their techniques. But for now, like a good American, I'll stay hopped up on coffee just to get through the afternoon.

### *the joys of public transportation*

While we were in the States, I will admit that I enjoyed driving a car. Not just a little bit, but a lot. Getting to roll down my window and sing En Vogue's "Free Your Mind" while bopping my shoulders around like I'm putting on a shirt that's too tight is both exhilarating and freeing. In the midst of rhythmically bobbing my hand through the window, I get to relax and breathe for a minute. We've been back in China for a few months now and I've enjoyed getting back into the public transportation game. While driving a car is fun for me, it also feeds into my independent and introverted tendencies. Sometimes having to rub shoulders with strangers is helpful in reminding me to get out and talk with people.

Only five people are supposed to fit in a taxi at one time. This poses a bit of a problem for our family of seven. When my youngest daughter was smaller, we took the ambush approach. Jackson and a couple of kids would stand on the curb, waving down a taxi the rest of us casually strolled near the bushes. Once he got in the front seat, I was commanded to, "Go, go, go!" Staying low, we attacked the backseat and slammed the door shut, leaving the taxi driver completely defenseless. We had just used guerrilla warfare tactics to secure a ride. We couldn't stand together to get a taxi because one look at our family and the drivers would nod and wave us off like we do to those poor survey people in the mall. At this point the taxi driver either laughs or tells us that we have too many people and we must get out. We usually guilt him into letting us stay by telling him he couldn't abandon us to the street with all these little children. We have no dignity whatsoever.

The bus system here is very efficient and is one of the main modes of transportation. Because we no longer have babies that we can tuck away on our laps, our ambushing days are over. We now have to hail two taxis. This is not only expensive, but time consuming, so we usually hop on a bus. The buses remind me of when I was a child and I filled up empty summer afternoons by shoving marshmallow after fluffy marshmallow in my mouth until I gagged, threw up, and did it again. On each humid bus rolling by, there will be bags, arms, hats, and babies clumped together like canned fruit stuck inside a cherry Jell-O mold. With each turn and sway of the bus, we move in one gelatinous motion. And within a few minutes, somehow we get squeezed out the door just in time for our stop.

Another amazing phenomenon is the train system. From most major cities, you can board a train and land in another location fairly easily. But there are different classes of train cars that will make your journey look very different. The high-speed trains are mostly filled with middle to upper class passengers and have some semblance of order. The tall beautiful stewardesses bring you a bottle of water and take hundreds of pictures of your children with their cell phones. There is a lady that comes through the cabins every few hours to sweep and collect trash. There are seats and rows similar to what you would find in the economy section of the airplane. No smoking is allowed and normally the aisles are cleared of people. If the cabin is full, you can buy a standing ticket and just squat in a corner the entire ride.

In contrast are the slower trains that resemble cattle cars. The times I have taken these, eight-year old shepherd boys shook my hand and goats ate the moss that had collected on our cabin from lack of movement. The train stops every hour to exhale and inhale more passengers. Like preparing to dive to the bottom of a deep pool, the train takes in one long extended breath to allow yet another person onboard. Once you are inside these cattle cars, the air is pulsing with people and congested with luggage. Middle-aged men are smoking and spitting wrinkled sunflower seed shells onto the ground; the older women are peeling grapes with their teeth and opening plastic bags of chicken feet. Generational guilt has led the younger people to stand and allow their elders to sit in the coveted seats. The train is crammed full of people, spilling arms and necks out the windows. When you know that you might get stuck in the middle of a crowded aisle, there are precautions you must take:

You don't eat or drink until you arrive at your destination. If you decide to do such frivolous things, you will find yourself having to cut through layers of people to find a bathroom and then once you get there, you cannot be *so* sure that you would actually want to enter it.

You want to stand near somebody approximately your height. At about hour 22, Mother Nature is going to tell you to close your eyes and sleep. But because you can do nothing but stand, you have to lay your head on a stranger's shoulders. There is a specific balance you must strike as you carefully lean into the person behind you and lay your head on the stranger to the right.

Your must bend and exercise your legs at appropriate intervals to aid in blood circulation. If you don't, after thirty-six hours of standing and swaying in the train, your legs will start to ache and swell and walking will be a pipe dream when you get to your destination.

Every year around the time of Chinese New Year we have friends who embark on these perilous journeys. They will spend thirty-plus hours standing on a train before boarding a long distance bus for five hours in order to get back to their villages to celebrate with family. But missing this celebration would be worse than any experience they might have on these cattle cars.

Our family has grown to love the high speed and sleeper trains. The sleeper trains stack up 3 skinny bunk beds into cubbyholes that you pile into with strangers. I realize that this might seem creepy, but it's like a slumber party with a train full of smoking middle-aged Chinese men. Ok that still sounds creepy. But we find them comfortable and quaint. About 8 p.m., the work clothes are tucked away and suddenly the entire compartment is decked out in cotton pajamas. The soft lull of the engine and the patient creaking of the tracks quietly sing you to sleep. When you get to your destination, a stewardess comes by and shakes your leg. It's fun to stretch out, relax, and then simply arrive at your destination.

## cultural musings on birds

I'm always looking for ways to describe the vast sea of cultural differences we find ourselves swimming in. This one dives into what we value.

One of the hobbies of the older and much, much WISER generation (you're welcome, Mom) is to take care of birds. You see the old people take them for walks, whistle to them, carry them on long wooden poles, teach them to gamble, and whatever else they can do to fill up a 16-hour day.

I've asked around and have found out that most people here believe that by getting a bird and putting it into a cage, they are protecting and loving the birds from the predators and evil elements that are found outside of cages. They will tell me that inside the cage, the birds are safe and well fed. Outside of the cage, they can be eaten, hit or abused. The cage offers safety, security and consistency. This is the most loving thing the caretaker can provide for the birds.

Now we Americans on the other hand, see a bird in a cage (I realize that some Americans still have birds as pets, but I just don't think they rank up there with dogs, cats, or even ferrets), and think "Fly away! Fly away while your owner is changing your newspapers! Escape, find your soulmate and make happy birdie babies while sipping lemonade in a Florida retirement community."

Fundamentally, we believe that birds were meant to fly and soar, to scale new heights and experience the world from a view that nobody else gets to see. We value the freedom that birds have. We see the cage as oppressive and stale.

Neither one is good or evil, just two different perspectives on the same thing...a cage. But it unpacks a lot culturally for both sides. Depending on your desires for the bird, one can be viewed as loving while the other one cruel.

### becoming a US ambassador to China

Our first few years in China were spent teaching English at a university in Northern China. After teaching, we decided that we would head into language school fulltime. I optimistically strolled into the first day of language school about five years ago, excited at having just moved back to China and getting to actually study the language instead of pantomiming my way through the day. I had these dreams of being so proficient at Chinese that the United Nations would be offering me a job by my second semester. As I took my seat among the other students, I quickly realized that my husband and I were the only Americans in the class. The other students came from South Korea, Japan and Russia. When the teacher opened her mouth my brain simultaneously left on vacation to Guam. It didn't matter that this was first semester Chinese, the teacher simply rattled on and on while I scampered to catch up. I felt like a three-year-old child holding onto their father's hand while he was jogging. No...sprinting. My little legs moved and moved, but all I could do was trip over my own two feet, fall and bloody both my knees.

Both my Korean and Japanese friends had studied Chinese growing up. The two Russian girls had already mastered several languages and had been studying at this university for a few semesters. I reminded them that I was American and that we

Americans have a principle of just making everyone else learn English. And if we do study another language, it's either Spanish or French because well, they are closest to English.

After about a week of feeling like I was running on a treadmill in a darkroom, not quite sure I was going anywhere but getting really tired in the process, I realized something: the teacher was also speaking Korean! That was why all my Korean friends laughed at appropriate places, answered questions and participated in group activities. I just nodded and hoped she didn't ask me a question.

One day, a young teacher decided to throw me a lifeline and use a new English phrase she had just learned. Unfortunately, a lot of the English instruction over here happens by watching "Desperate Housewives" and "Prison Break." And we then have to instruct our friends that calling a taxi driver a bastard is not actually appropriate to do in real life. Well, this teacher was really excited to use her new English phrase with her class that day. She told us about the word 'tan yi tan' (which actually means to have a discussion or a chat). She turned around and smiled as if to prod us to be amazed at the forthcoming English sentence. She loudly declared, "Tan yi tan means FRIENDLY INTERCOURSE! All of us here are having FRIENDLY INTERCOURSE!" She was so excited about getting the entire sentence out correctly that she said it over and over again, repeating the phrase "friendly intercourse," while writing it in huge block letters on the chalk board. It was as if I had been transported to freshman year homeroom. I was laughing so hard I had to fake choke just to leave the classroom. Of course nobody else in the classroom got the humor in all of it, they simply took copious notes and nodded in agreement.

The Chinese system of learning language falls right in line with the rest of their educational system. They require rote memorization. The way the written language is structured, you have to memorize hundreds of characters before you can read simple children's books. While I was able to teach my older son to start reading by three years old, there is no possibility of that for a Chinese child. They cannot just pick up a short book about yellow ducks and sound out the words. They either have the character memorized or they don't, and because each character is an actual word instead of a letter, they can't even guess. So when we Westerners stroll into Chinese language class with all 26 English letters in our language arsenal, we quickly realize we are up against a language of Goliath proportions.

Language school is hard. And it lingers. Just when you think you've nailed the language, someone asks you a question at the market and the only response you can muster up is, "What?" There is no completion to the task and God very rarely downloads Chinese into somebody, like Neo from the Matrix. Almost everyone I know has had to work painstakingly long hours to master a language. And the thing is, if God wanted me to have language quickly, He could give it to me over night. It's because of this simple truth, that God has chosen not to give me language overnight, that I am even remotely joyful about the whole process. Apparently God wants me to grow and mature in the learning of a new language. He wants me to slow down and appreciate the cultural heritage embedded in the characters. He wants me to feel the pain of being illiterate so that my time with farmers with a 4th grade education would be spent in admiration instead of frustration. And He wants to remind me that it is Him at work here, not me.

The first few Chinese classes are spent becoming familiar with the sounds, followed quickly by learning the order in which to draw the strokes that make the characters. They then send us home with the assignment of learning 50 characters each week. Not just memorizing its meaning, but legibly writing each character on a large sheet of graph paper. Watching my friends write their characters with absolute artistry made me deeply wish that I could be good at it. But the amount of time I would spend learning how to compose each character correctly is about 100 times what I've got right now. I can read the characters and send a text message, but to sit down and scribble out a character requires me to call my nine-year-old daughter into the room. Because she goes to a Chinese school half of the day, her characters look like perfect fonts.

Each character has evolved over time. The history and stories behind them is fascinating. For example, the word for family is 家 (jia). The top portion of the character represents cover or a roof. The bottom half is the character for pig. So to have a pig and a roof over your head would be to have a satisfied family.

The character for good is 好 (hao). It is the combination of the character for woman and the character for child. To have a mother with a child is the essence of good in Chinese.

The ancient character for boat 船 (chuan) is the combination of small boat, the number eight, and mouth or person. Some believe that this could be representative of the ark holding Noah and his family. While there is some debate over the watermarkings of Genesis in ancient Chinese script, I think it's at least worth considering that God had revealed himself to the Chinese thousands of years ago.

The written language is filled with stories of the values that the Chinese have held dear for thousands of years. Writing them by hand is truly an art form. As we have learned to read, we have come to a better understanding not only of the history of our friends, but the worldview that makes them tick.

## a morning's declaration

I love hearing birds sing early in the morning. It's as if they are waking up the day with praises of proclamation to the King. They are heralding new mercies lifted in by the sun. The birds are fervent in their trumpeting because they know we won't want to miss the parading of grace that will be rolled out to start our morning. Valiantly, the sun pushes back the defensive posturing of the night. Never can night push back, the sun merely retreats for a time. The volition of the sun commands the day. Upon it's coming, kings are stirred into motion and countries are bound to its whims. To deny the power of the sun is to smugly declare your own throne. God is King and to deny Him as such is to vote yourself in as commander of a Kingdom devoid of democracy.

He will gently unfold the flowers in spring; majestically shake stars from their blanket of day; twirl tornadoes across lonely plains; retreat legions of bears in the war of winter.

He is a gracious, powerful, temperate, commander who demands attention and full obedience, but not simply to display His strong-arm. Our obedience comes as we see that victory is always His. Whether through patience or pursuit, God wins. Every time. As His people, our souls should rise each morning in triumphant pursuit of hearing His commands. There should be victory in our voices and expectancy in our ears as He comes to proclaim that He made today and declared it good.

# Squatty Potties and Other Realities

"Before you criticize someone, you should walk a mile in their shoes. That way when you criticize them, you are a mile away from them and you have their shoes."

Anonymous

*Life over here has stretched how I define "normal." Just because I eat with a fork and speak English doesn't make that a standard for normal. We are learning to listen to the differences, observe the reasonings, and love the normal of those around us.*

## accosted by ming dynasty

Several years ago, my husband was teaching English at a university in Northern China. I was at home with my two kids and studied Chinese one hour a week. I naively thought I could speak Chinese with that meager amount of studying. That was, until I stepped outside and tried to communicate with a phrase other than, "I need to buy lettuce." When people paused, implying they had just asked me a question, my default response was to tell them where we were from. They might have been asking me directions to a hotel or what I thought of the weather, but I simply smiled and responded by telling them "Yes, I am American."

One day, I had taken my kids and one of their friends out to play at a local park. When you read "local park" don't think slides, monkey bars and climbing walls. Think retirement plaza with exercise equipment and poles to beat your legs on. Visualize impromptu games of poker played while sitting on small pieces of newspaper spread over concrete slabs.

As I was chasing the kids around the park, dodging puddles of pee from the toddlers wandering around with their grandparents, I ran into a man who was a local icon-Ming Dynasty. That's not actually his name, but that's what we called him. He was around 80 and had a long glistening silver beard. He still wore his Mao era blue jumpsuit and sauntered around campus with a wooden cane. He was the master Yoda. Because of all of this, we decided that Ming Dynasty was an appropriate name for the guy. Older men are to be feared and respected in China. There is a reverent glow that follows that generation of men. Feeling the glow, I walked past Ming Dynasty and said hello. Leaving skid marks with his cane, he shuffled towards me. Quickly. Preparing my mind to speak Chinese, I said "Hello!"

He cut straight to asking me if all these children were mine. I tried answering him, but it seemed as if he really just wanted to ask me this question: "Are you still nursing that one?" He was pointing at my 2 ½ year old son.

He wasn't sure if I understood his question, so he puckered his lips and made a loud smacking sound with his toothless mouth. Still not sure if I understood, he reached out his hands and gave my little 'milk factories' a quick squeeze. I will tell you that all of this happened in slow motion. I swear I had no idea why the hand was encroaching my orbit, but it certainly didn't come to mind that I would be groped by ol' Ming Dynasty. I smiled awkwardly and then he threw me the pucker, smacking routine again. Thinking that he just wasn't getting through to the foreign lady, his long wrinkly hands swept across my chest to grab the other side. The only word I knew that was both appropriate and in Chinese was "NO!"

I shuffled back a few steps and could only laugh at the whole scene. He really was not trying to be inappropriate; he was simply asking me a question and trying to help me be a good mother. I gathered my little chicks and we made an excuse to return home three and half minutes after getting to the park.

## circus of sellers

I love the way we shop here. While there are some larger corporate grocery stores in most major cities, I still prefer to shop at local markets. These markets aren't always official sites, but perhaps just an older lady's wool blanket spread full of shoelaces, toilet brushes and a watermelon. As you turn the corner to enter a more official type of market, you are paraded into a kaleidoscope for your senses. You become engulfed within the big canopy of steam rising from the frying tofu and boiling duck eggs that forces your hurry to pull up a stool and sit awhile.

Shaping each alley is a splattering of small forts draped in dangling white lights. The bulbs are strung across the alley in a web of comforting chaos. The forts are covered in crooked blue and red tarps stretching over their six-by-six foot stalls. Each seller shouts out what he or she is attempting to get you to purchase. As you walk through a tight alley and avoid bumping the raw pig's hooves that are hung from a two by four with a rusty hook, your mind becomes whimsically aware that you have been transported away from the modern world. The squawking chickens greet you "good morning," and flopping fish splash the dust from your shoes. Like the ring master, the smell of rice noodles and steamed meat buns lure you to the back of the marketplace. Retreating from the bustle of the morning, the early afternoon draws women inside their sturdy umbrellas to cross-stitch or gossip about the foreigners with five kids.

The men roll up their baggy shirts and lay their heads on peach crates to sleep for the next hour and a half. The market culture is notably slower and more jovial than walking through a grocery store. Vendors are trading a bowl of noodles for a bag of ripened mangoes. The old men are toting their plastic bags filled with one green pepper and a dead fish. No body is looking to get rich or open up a new Sam's Club with their genius marketing strategies. They are all just looking to make enough money to close out the day with a meal on the table and a mind full of stories to share.

Because my kids have blonde hair, one of them is black and they all speak Chinese, we get given all types of free things while we wander through markets; usually it's fruit or some type of warm flat bread. But the price they pay is a head pat, a cell phone picture, an arm rub and usually a comment about how little they are wearing.

Several years ago, I stopped by my favorite fruit vendor to pick up some apples and pears. While I was negotiating with the vendor, Corbin (who was only 11 months at the time) had been sitting quietly in his stroller behind me. I soon realized why he was so content. The 90-year-old matriarch of the fruit stand was sitting next to my son mumbling toothless Chinese and looking delighted. As I watched, I realized that she was licking her lips. Her lips were sticky because she had just finished gnawing a large purple grape, regurgitating it and feeding it to my son like a caring mother bird. He swallowed it quickly and was soon asking for another one. Reflexes like a puma, I intercepted this primal feeding of my son and politely asked her to bag up the rest of the grapes. I consoled myself with the fact that this frail woman was 90, therefore indicating that she probably didn't have some terminal disease that she would have so lovingly passed along to my son. She smiled and waved as I ran back home looking for Lysol to spray on his tongue.

## Chinese funerals

The low pressing instruments of mourning interrupted today's early stillness. I can still hear the trumpets and pan flutes gathering their bravado to sing the words the family can't speak. The music swirls around my apartment complex conducting a soul to the afterlife and directing those around to march forward until death. Small pockets of people have gathered around to pay their tributes and reunite with old friends. Daughters are holding onto their mothers as if age will give wisdom by virtue of proximity. The more intimate parties are inside, bundled around the body trying to make sense of what they have lost. For some it has been a father who has customarily kept all things together. Maybe a mother who provided the matriarchal gauze wrapped tightly around the wounds of a childhood. For others it is a sister whose famous fried dumplings will leave a noticeable hole at the Chinese New Year dinner table. For many Chinese, this is it. The reds and blues that color our day are all there is to be enjoyed in a lifetime. After that, you simply cease. One day, you stop breathing, your heart slows its pounding, and then you are done. The belief system of materialism leaves little room for an afterlife. You merely expand your lungs to take in the minutes you have on earth, and then one day you lose your ability to breathe.

Tubas, trumpets, bagpipes, pan flutes, and huge barrel drums are enmeshed in song outside the mourner's apartment. The music has been playing for three hours and will probably continue until after lunch, when the call to rest and the afternoon's work remind us that we are still here. As the music rolls through the air, it's as if the credits are streaming down the screen of a movie filled with melancholic dialogue and tragic endings. The fortissimos are soft and gradual and minor notes seem to be wrapped rightfully around each rest and refrain. As each song is played, the family is one note closer to the end of the playlist; one note closer to living out tomorrow what today's reality struck them with. While the instruments are being packed away and flowers loaded back on the truck, their lives will have to continue on. They will be required to keep running, no matter how hard it is to breathe.

The first time I saw a Chinese funeral, I couldn't help but sit down and take it all in. Death seems to be one of the only situations that will turn a godless eye to the possibility of an afterlife. Most of the funeral customs are done in public as to require even casual passersby to pay tributes and feel the loss suffered by their neighbors.

Whenever you see a truck packed with hula-hoop-sized flower displays, you know that they are on their way to a funeral. The neon colored flowers are tucked neatly around in a circle, framing a large Chinese character. Usually it's this character:

奠 (dian), symbolizing a ceremonial mourning.

The families will sometimes be wearing long white robes with white hoods, which coming from an American background adds a little uneasiness. But this white uniform represents mourning because white is the color representing death here, not black. Oftentimes the flower displays will be put at the entrance to a tiny shrine that has been put together to honor the recently deceased. The family members will also place large paper replicas of servants to give to their loved ones in the after life. On the floor, family will burn incense, money, and paper cell phones to make sure their family member is well equipped after passing away. While many Chinese don't believe in a formal afterlife, they participate in these rituals as a last ditch effort of hope. The families put up small stools to sit on because the funeral site should be manned at all times. We have even heard stories of families hiring mourners. These are people hired to weep and mourn in a more dramatic way to signify the depth of loss that their community feels, especially if the family is small. Depending on where you are living here, funerals can look very different. In the more rural settings, there are typically more sacrifices for your ancestor's afterlife.

The funeral I watched this morning was for someone of much reputation. The casket was draped drearily with a thick red comforter and was being carried slowly by the sons and uncles of the family. A band marched out with fireworks booming behind. The heavy casket was slid into a moderate sized van, decked out in cut flowers and stuffy carpets.

As the van pulled away, I recognized the fear embedded in the lines wrapped softly around the widow's eyes. The sole provider the family was now lying lifeless in the back of a van. Promises of a daughter going to the big city to study were now defined by a simple question mark. The flowers had been placed back in the truck and the music was now playing at another funeral down the street. The ceremony was finished, but the unknown had just begun.

## contracts schmontracts

As we negotiated with the landlords in our new city in Southern China, I was reminded of a little word that actually has very little meaning here: contract. We have contracts here in the motherland, but nobody abides by them. They simply draw them up and pound them with a big red stamp and pretend like it will hold if you need to refer back to it in the future. In the last apartment we lived in up North, we had a minor run-in with our landlord. Because we blew through our time frame on coming back home to China, our lease at our old apartment had expired while we sat in the U-S-of-A.

At that point, we had to rely on our generous friends and their desire to be sanctified. Our landlord seized the opportunity to tell our friends that we had "verbally" agreed to leave everything we bought to put in the house and to pay to have the place repainted. These things were not agreed to verbally, but he saw that we were stuck because our friends were doing this on our behalf. With much back and forth, we told the landlord that we weren't giving him what he wanted.

There was nothing in our contract stating his demands, but that didn't matter. He went on to tell us that he was a high powered government official and that if we didn't give him what he demanded, then he was going to call the Mafia and have them take care of our stuff and our friends. At first, we chuckled at the fact that the government official was going to take care of things via hiring his Mafia friends. Then we realized that he was serious and we knew we had lost the negotiation. We didn't want the Mafia messing with our friends. It's one thing for them to take my curtains; it's another to physically threaten people we cared about. I did the Tae Bo videos as a freshman in college, but I'm pretty sure my upper cut, forward kick sequence won't be helpful when taking on members of the Mafia.

In the end we lost some of our stuff. Our friends moved our things out late into the night because they were nervous that the landlord would lock up our apartment and we'd never see any of it ever again. They totally pulled a Macgyver and moved with much stealth to get our things out. I was serious when I said that they earned some major treasures in heaven through all of this. At the end of the day, I was reminded that it's just stuff. And if it devastated me too much to lose any of it, then I was probably attached to it in an unhealthy manner anyway.

It is just stuff.

### sheep placenta lotion

While walking through the grocery store yesterday I was looking to buy lotion for Joi (who is very much not white) that didn't have a whitening agent in it. According to the Chinese, the whiter your skin, the prettier you are. My Chinese friends always compliment me on how white and pasty I am. I remind them that that is not at all a compliment to an American.

As I was looking in the lotion section, I happened upon sheep placenta lotion. My first thought was "Why would I want to rub placenta on my hands, nevermind a sheep's placenta?" I forwent the lotion and moved on. As I moseyed through the grocery store, I was reminded at how a very common item in the United States can be so different here. Take grocery shopping for example. The aisles are filled with green tea Oreos, seaweed Lays, coffee gum, green pea ice cream, apple vinegar drinks and hairy pig's legs. And while these things are odd and quite frankly, disgusting, our kids enjoy most of them.

My husband and I have to be very careful about what items we label as weird. To our children, snacking on shrimp flakes or a vacuum packed chicken claw is totally normal. For example, a few years ago, we traveled back to the States and were having dinner with friends. Our oldest daughter was only 4 at the time. She was excited when on the children's menu she read "chicken fingers" on the children's menu. When the spritely young waitress brought her meal and put it down on the table, our daughter looked up in utter confusion and said, "Mommy, these aren't chicken fingers. Where are the claws?"

"Well, sweetie," I replied, trying not to laugh, "here in America, they don't actually eat chicken fingers. You see, Americans like their meat to look like meat and not the actual animal from which their meal came."

She looked at me puzzled and said "That's weird. They shouldn't call these chicken fingers if they aren't fingers."

"You're right, honey. I don't know why they are called chicken fingers."

This is our children's world. Eating noodles for breakfast, hearing fireworks during the day, peeing on the streets, eating fermented eggs and picking corn-flavored ice cream instead of chocolate brings comfort to them. It's hard to know how to navigate these waters as a parent, especially when it is so different from the suburbia childhood of both my husband and me.

We are realizing that we need to be slow to label things. That what is different to us is familiar to them. We are also learning to keep our commentary about the strange smells, spitting grandmothers and cultural habits to ourselves. Oftentimes, if we don't understand things, we stick them in a negative box. It helps us feel in control. When we don't actively try and understand the why's or how's of people, then everything becomes negative and we grow cold to those around us. My husband and I have to discipline ourselves to take a strange situation or person and actively try to make sense of it.

For instance, around most parks here you will see the bottom half of the trees painted a stark white color. This has perplexed me since day one. I have inquired about this random cultural habit of painting the trees. I have been told it helps people not run into them with their bikes or cars or that it keeps them warm. This made no sense to me, so my initial thought was, "That's so illogical! Is painting a tree half white really going to stop a car from careening into it?!" Every time I saw a painted tree I had a negative cultural thought about the whole thing. That is, until a friend saw one being painted in the States. Apparently they were using clear paint, but painting nonetheless. My friend knew of my consternation about the painted trees and asked the person why they were painting them. The person told her that it's to keep bugs out. That the bugs can't get into the tree with the paint on it and by the time they are halfway up, they figure there isn't a tree to be eaten, so they leave. That made more sense to me. I'm so glad I figured that out, but I'm ashamed of the posture I took while not understanding. The Lord loves to show me my pride and expose my desire to knock others down. I hate it, but the Lord is helping me to slow down my placement of people and things into negative categories and that is always a positive thing.

## scabies

Not only did we bring Joi home from Ethiopia but we also packed a family of scabies to join us back in China. These little visitors were discovered the day Jackson went out of town for a week. Lovely.

Scabies oh scabies from where did you come?
We're itching all over, toes to our thumbs.

They are small and pesky, those tiny white mites
With no discretion, our bodies they bite.

The doctors say 'nah, it just looks rashy'
For THAT diagnosis I paid you my cashy?

Oh doctors, oh doctors, you misdiagnosed,
Apparently, you didn't look very close.

The couch has been vacuumed,
The bathroom's been scrubbed
Three days of smearing medicine
Then we're jumpin' in the tub.

The sheets are all washed,
The floors have been swept.
Bleach is abounding
And Mommy has wept.

It's been a long week, scabies my friends
But your stay at my house must come to an end.

You see, this week, my husband's been gone
Babies are sick and I've been up 'til dawn.

So I'm afraid you'll have to take your bags and get packing.
I'm tired of your games and your late night attacking.

I'm tired of your presence, your marks, and your stay
It's *zai jian*, *man zou*, good bye and good day!

- *zai jian* means *good-bye* and *man zou* means *go slowly* in Chinese. Both are common ways of saying good-bye here.

*bloodwork again*

We just got back from a family trip to Hong Kong and Guangzhou. Our visas require all of us to leave the country every 90 days. On this particular visa run, we decided to take a trip to Hong Kong Disney. If you live in Asia, going to Hong Kong Disney is a rite of passage. It's like getting your wings. We had a blast hanging out with princesses and Buzz Lightyear for the day.

We took the two-hour train from Hong Kong into Guangzhou. In Guangzhou, we would be renewing three of our kid's passports and doing a medical check-up for our five-year-old daughter, Grace. Everything was going too smoothly. My pessimistic skin was just waiting for something to burn us. And sure enough, our last two days in Guangzhou were spent running back and forth to the hospital. When we left the States, Grace still had some elevated eosinophil (a white blood cell in the immune system) counts. Both she and Joi just couldn't seem to shake the parasite that was camped out in their bodies. This was the entire reason our time in the States was prolonged. While the medicine eradicated them from Joi's system, at the time, Grace's weren't high enough to do a treatment. Even though Grace's levels went down a little, our doctors wanted another blood test to be done 3-6 months after getting back to China.

In order to see a doctor with any type of medical training, we needed to travel to a bigger city. This usually requires several taxis, trains and even an airplane or two. I wrestled with the Lord regarding the medical security of my family before we moved over here. I realized that a simple thing like an asthma attack could kill my child because we couldn't get to good medical help fast enough. We know a family who lived in a remote African village for many years. Their healthy 16-year-old son died in their home after suffering a relatively normal asthma attack. I worked with the Lord long and hard on this and He finally brought my heart of a place of submission and trust that His will is always good. Even if that meant the death of one of my children.

We did the blood tests and the doctor sat down to tell us the news. Having the doctor organize her papers and settle in for a conversation is never a good start to blood results. The doctor explained that Grace's white blood cell count was elevated again and we would need to do some stool samples to check for parasites. This was Thursday at 4:30 pm. We were scheduled to fly home Friday at 4:30 pm. The hospital we were at had doctors trained in the States, so we felt confident that she knew what she was doing.

But assuming that we couldn't get three stool samples in 12 hours, the doctor wrote out what we should do at our local hospital back home. Honestly, the only thing I could think of was how local hospitals remind me of a rodeo. Except that you triple the people and there are no cattle. Just people running around and going crazy trying to lasso a doctor to talk to. There are no lines, just each man for himself. And you have to pay for every different step of the process before the doctor will talk to you. You pay, run back, throw your receipt at the doctor, and talk loudly about whatever ails you. If you are not loud, pushy, and persistent, you will not leave the hospital. Ever.

This entire scene played out in my mind as our doctor wrote the instructions down. I'm pretty sure I shortened my life by 8 years just thinking of how stressful that would be. And then to do it three times. The backs of my knees started sweating while my small intestines did a sleeper hold on my stomach. It made me desperately persistent to try and get the samples done in the next 12 hours.

Remember, we had been eating Western food in Hong Kong for every meal. Bread, cheese and sausage didn't bode well for getting my five-year-old daughter to produce three stool samples in a 12-hour period. This same daughter is afraid of dogs, kittens, and dolphins that will eat her skirt. And here I was about to use an enema in a noisy coffee shop. I'm sure this will come up in counseling later on in her life. But I kept the rodeo scene fresh in my mind at each bathroom attempt. I was not going to do this at a local hospital at home.

The Lord got my girl's bowels moving and we knocked out two samples the first night. Empowered to get this accomplished, I resorted to prune juice, apples, and plastic gloves.

It was 10 a.m. on the day we were supposed to fly home and...nothing. She was trying so hard. We had to check out of the hotel, running to public bathrooms all over the city trying to find a toilet with a seat. I won't go into a lengthy explanation here, but trust me, collecting a stool sample is easier on a toilet with a seat than on a squatty potty. The only toilet with a seat to be found was at Starbucks. This also came in handy as I put the samples in a plastic bag and transported them in Starbucks cups to the hospital.

The clock struck 11:15 a.m. We were scheduled to get on a bus at 1:00 pm to get to the airport. I began to sweat like Jack Black in summertime. The plastic gloves finally had to go places that they didn't really want to go. Still nothing. I resigned to the fact that Grace and I would have to stay in Guangzhou, waiting for her to go to the bathroom. I then realized that there was a small pharmacy across the street. I ran over there and told the pharmacist that I needed something for my daughter's clogged stomach. I told her, "I don't want medicine, I want a tool!" I didn't know the Chinese word for "enema," but between pantomiming the action and using bathroom words, she got the point. I paid and ran back to Starbucks. I figured we own a solid 4 shares of Starbucks stock, therefore I had certainly earned the right to give my daughter an enema in their bathrooms.

I will skip this part, but just know that the enema worked. I sprinted with my Starbucks cup that was carrying my daughter's third and final stool sample. I had 1 hour to drop it off at the hospital and get to the bus. Taxi drivers were changing shifts, so it took me 20 minutes to find someone to take me. Once one stopped, I lurched myself into his backseat and told him that it was an emergency and to get to the hospital. Many taxi drivers are fairly new to the driving world, so it's rarely a smooth pleasant ride. They haven't quite grasped the whole gas/brake balance and so they end up tapping out "Battle Hymn of the Republic" on their gas pedals as we ride along. Nauseous, I finally arrived at the hospital, threw the sample at the nurse, and darted out the front door.

Panting, I got to the bus station and we loaded up. Now we just had to wait for the results. We were grateful that we figured this out and hopeful that since we dealt with this exact same thing with Joi that a diagnosis would come fairly quickly.

## *squatty potties*

Not gonna lie, I like the squatty potty. If you have never seen one, it's essentially a glorified hole in the ground that you straddle, squat, and do your thing. I have grown to love this way of taking care of business. You just don't ever want to make the mistake of losing your balance. This has happened to me on a few occasions, all when I was pregnant. I'm pregnant often, so this has occurred several times over the span of the last six years. Your center of gravity shifts so much during pregnancy… as does your coordination.

My favorite was a time that we were attending a good friend's wedding out in the countryside. Her family didn't have indoor plumbing, so we had to face the elements and head to the outhouse. Not to worry, there was a long stick with a bucket attached to the end to remove the packages left by the users. My friend was mildly embarrassed by their home when my husband, three kids and I (being eight months pregnant) came to spend some time with them leading up to the wedding. She wanted us to be comfortable, so she put a pretty little light blue plastic bowl in the corner of our shared room. It was so thoughtful of her that I didn't want to explain how hard it is for a woman who is 8-months pregnant to aim her business into a saucer.

Every few hours I had to get up to use the facilities. My family all shared a common bed, so every time I lifted my legs in the air to get my pregnant rompus out of bed, I woke somebody up. I eventually made it to the saucer and squatted like a sumo wrestler in starting position. But what do you do with the bowl when you are done? I dragged it outside and dumped it in her green bean garden because it was closest. It was soon after this experience that I suggested wearing adult diapers to bed so that I could take care of things swiftly and without much disruption to my sleep.

At many Western restaurants here, they have a sign posted telling people to not stand and squat on the Western toilets. It explains that people must sit down on the seat and take care of things.

As I think of the public restrooms in America, I will say that they win in the cleanliness category. I have just never been able to navigate the whole levitate while going thing that most women have an instinct for. I was absent when God passed out that skill in the creation line. And sitting down on a seat that is still warm makes my toes curl up in my boots. I'd rather just squat.

## *the big test*

Next week holds the test that Chinese families prepare for from the time their child could sit up independently. It's called the *gao kao*, which is Mandarin for "big test." The *gao kao* is like the SAT only much more important. In order to get into college here, you have to have a high enough score on the *gao kao*. All throughout high school, you work late nights and memorize entire chapters just to prepare your mind to take that test. You see, if you do poorly on the test, you don't go to college. Period. The day before the test you could have been the valedictorian of your entire high school, but that is all for not if you don't get a good score on the *gao kao*. Each college here is ranked with an A, B, or C type of leveling. Once you get your test back, your score is slotted into the appropriate category. The highest scorings will go to 'A' ranked universities and so on. Universities don't look at a high school transcript or a list of extracurricular activities; they simply evaluate your *gao kao* score. Last year, more than 9.57 million students competed for 6.57 million places in China's universities and colleges. That left three million students who had to either try again the next year or find a job in their hometown.

You get one shot at the *gao kao*. It takes place your senior year during the first week of June. The test only happens in the course of a few days, so if you are sick or your mother dies, too bad. Many students actually end up going to live at an extended family member's house for the month prior to the test. That way, the student could be undistracted in their studies. We have heard of student's parents passing away while they were off studying, but nobody told them until after the test for fear of derailing their concentration. Benjamin Siegel with Time Magazine reported that, "In Tianjin, China's third-biggest metropolis, doctors reportedly prescribed birth control pills to female test-takers whose parents feared that an untimely period would prove distracting. In Sichuan Province in southwestern China, students studied in a hospital, hooked up to oxygen containers, in hopes of improving their concentration."

While each province has modified the way the testing is done, for the most part, it takes place over the span of two to three days. After you take the *gao kao*, you can list a few universities to get your scores sent to. If your scores don't reach those standards than you just don't get into any university. In some provinces, you will be allowed to list a few schools after having received your scores. Chinese, Mathematics, and a foreign language (usually English) are standard on every test. Biology, Physics, and Chemistry are the choices for any future Math/Engineering majors. You are required to pick at least one of these subjects to test in if you are wanting to be a Science major. If you are looking to Humanities, you are required to test in History, Geography, or Political Education.

The tension surrounding this test can be felt for months prior to it actually taking place. We have received advertisements at the kindergarten for DVDs promising high *gao kao* scores or special drinks that will aid in giving our student a *gao kao* advantage even starting at three years old. The pressure of this test has also brought about creative ways of cheating. Students using high tech walkie talkies or radio transmission have all been caught and told they will never be able to take the test again. To curb potential cheaters, Siegel writes, "Exam authors are confined to secret compounds while the test is being written, while the printing is carried out by inmates at maximum-security prisons."

After your scores come back, the sections are divided into your proficiencies. For example, if you did well on the physics section, then you would be slotted in as a physics major. If that department is full, your second best scores would be looked at. The students do get a little say in what they pick, but not much. Most of our university friends tell us that they don't like their major, but that's what the school gave them because of their *gao kao* scores.

I have always been a horrible test taker. I cannot imagine my future riding all on one test that I am sure would seal my fate selling lamb shiskabobs on the side of the street. The mounting pressure of this test has made education here frantic. Parents are in a panic to prepare their children for this one momentous day. And for those poor students who worked hard and got great grades but failed to perform on the *gao kao*? They end up deflated and discouraged at wasting their lives.

### wanting to be black

I just got back from working out and I realized something about my choice of music. I usually keep my mp3 player on shuffle, so I range from pre-pubescent vegetables to Christian rap. When the rap comes blaring into my ears, it's an involuntary action for my lips to pucker like I'm kissing the window and my hips to move in a punk-like swagger. This was a bit awkward as I was walking through my parent's very upper class, quaint little suburban neighborhood.

I'm going to lay all my cards out on the table and tell you all that I've always wanted to be black. And male. But I got over the male thing when I realized that wearing pants without underwear and peeing standing up don't work as an actual female. I've always loved my black friends and often named my plants more typically African American names, like L'ecretia.

Ever since I was in elementary school, I've wanted a black baby. I knew these sweet black girls that would sit with me on the bus and we would take turns doing each other's hair. The fact that I could take a strand of their hair, stick it straight up and it would stay was just about the coolest thing since mood rings and hyper colored t-shirts. So when we decided to adopt, my husband reminded me of my ethnic bias and told me to make sure I was objective in choosing a country to adopt from. I have to admit my prayers weren't totally objective.

We had a name for our daughter for about five years prior to adoption. We just didn't know that we were going to adopt nor that she would be from Ethiopia. Before we adopted her, I had several crazy moments where I went into the bedroom looking for our daughter. Even a week or two after our son was born, I would look around and had a sense that we were still missing a child. Already having four kids, it seemed a bit strange to think that our house was missing someone. I would go into rooms looking for her, but she didn't exist. I blamed it initially on pregnancy brain and then post-labor brain. But after about six months of it, I ran out of things to blame it on and decided that maybe God was trying to get through my thick cranium. When we decided on Ethiopia and found out that I would be receiving my black daughter whom I had dreamt about for the past 25 years, I suggested that we add an arbitrary apostrophe to her name. My husband pulled out the veto on that.

As we were adopting from Ethiopia but living in China, we knew there would be issues we would face that would be different than if we were still living permanently in the States. Very few people in China have seen a white person. Almost nobody has ever seen a black person, and if they have, it's because they watch the NBA. Within 6.5 seconds of being out I public, our daughter's hair usually gets grabbed and her skin gets touched to make sure the black doesn't come off. Fortunately, she is laid back about the whole thing. The funniest things happen though when the simple touching of her hand evolves into people opening their mouths to make statements like the ones below:

"Oh, I'm sure she will be a good basketball player one day because she is black!"

When she was one year old, her shoes came off while galloping around a playground. One of my closest friends who was intimately involved in helping us get our adoption paperwork done while living in China looked at me seriously commented, "Her shoes fell off. Oh, it must be because people in Africa don't wear shoes."

While looking at my black daughter and my white son together (who are about a year apart) we have had several people ask if they are twins. One pair of grandmothers was shocked at the discovery of multiracial twins. That is, until one hit the other playfully on the shoulder and told her "They aren't twins...look, the boy is taller!"

A friend was holding Joi when a woman walked up and asked her if she belonged to our family. After repeating our standard line of "Yes, she is our daughter," the lady came to her own conclusions about how a biracial family such as ours could exist in the modern world. Throwing her hypothesis out there for all to hear, she told us "Oh, I get it. The older she gets, the whiter and whiter she becomes." "Yep," I thought, "just like snow leopards."

The idea that non-white Americans actually do exist is a relatively new notion to most of our Chinese friends and neighbors. We are always getting asked where she is from, because certainly it's not from America. And when I tell them that she is also American, they decide to argue and tell me that she is black and therefore not American. Then I remind them that our President is black, to which they normally respond, "Obama is black?!"

My husband was being tutored in Chinese one afternoon when the tutor pulled out a picture of a rural village. The assignment was to describe the picture using some new vocabulary. He kept referring to the picture as an African village. The tutor kept correcting him by pointing to the goats and saying that the village is not in Africa. "See," she remarked, "the village isn't in Africa because the goats are white. There are not white goats in Africa, only black ones."

Most everyone is so sweet to her and not at all trying to be rude, they just have never seen a black person in real life. We try to patiently guide them into understanding the world and all its colors, but there are times we just shake our head and laugh because it seems the only appropriate thing to do.

*two years ago*

Two years ago this week, we were packing to move to a new city and preparing to pick up our youngest daughter from Ethiopia. It was with these things on my backdrop that I reflected on the grand spectacle that adoption can be. It is an open field that God fills with colors, textures, caverns and corners.

*(February 26, 2009)*

I love when God gives us a peek into His heart. Last month, we received our referral for our baby girl. For those of you unfamiliar with adoption, it's like the day you find out you are pregnant. There is joy, many tears and a sense of being overwhelmed that all happen simultaneously. With the referral, we get a picture and a name. No story, no explanation, just a child waiting.

I'm sitting in a corporate setting and experiencing the grace of worshipping with many saints. That's something my soul longs for here-corporate worship through song and prayer. I miss it dearly. So I'm sitting, listening, pleading with God, singing, and loving Jesus. All of the sudden, the picture of our little girl goes reeling through my mind over and over again. She's sitting in Ethiopia.... just waiting. We are her parents, but she has no idea, no concept and no way of finding us on her own. She can't up and walk out of her orphanage. She can't just escape her situation. She can't save herself. I get overwhelmed just reminiscing about this. God gave me this vision of her to remind me that this was EXACTLY who I was before Jesus came in and saved me. He rescued me from myself. He rescued me from my ungodly future. I was sitting there, not realizing I needed saving. I couldn't save myself. I couldn't pull myself up by my bootstraps. I couldn't earn my way to salvation. Just like our baby girl. She can't earn her way into our family. She can't do a thing until we go and get her.

About 12 years ago, God came and got me. He captured my heart, my soul, my future. And now I am His-forever. There is not a thing that our kids can do to separate us from them. Just as it is promised to God's children "nothing can separate you from the love of God." But first we have to be His child.

# Family Ties

"Behold, children are a heritage from the Lord, the fruit
of the womb a reward. Like arrows in the hand of
a warrior are the children of one's youth."

Psalm 127:3 (ESV)

*Because we moved here with children in tow, we get to receive the blessing of merging into the lives of the families around us. The mountain of differences in family dynamics between East and West is overwhelmingly large. But fundamentally, the differences fade into one similarity: we are all just trying to learn how to love each other well.*

## education: what's the point?

When we were in the States this past year, I was reminded of the fact that most Americans are scared to death of China. All the news reports are claiming that China is eons ahead of the US in terms of education. There was a book that came out last year called *Battle Hymn of the Tiger Mother*, written by Amy Chua. She is Chinese but is raising her two daughters in America and is married to a white Jewish man. The Wall Street Journal did a write up on the book in the fall of 2010 and just about made American parents everywhere jump out of their collective skin. I don't want to delve into educational theory and pedagogy because, quite simply, I am both under qualified and under-motivated to do the research. But I do know what my children have experienced while in national schools here.

Assimilating our kids into Chinese culture is of utmost importance to my husband and me. That means that the first half of their day is spent in a normal Chinese school where they pee in bowls, eat noodles for breakfast, learn songs called "My Teacher is Like my Mother," and then return home right before all their friends strip down naked to nap. The second half of their day is spent in home school. It is in the first half of their day that they experience a much different form of education than at home with mom.

Most Chinese children spend all day in school and most of the weekend taking extra classes. Every night, elementary aged students are spending 2-3 hours on homework. While this looks like a standard that Americans would never want to meet, the key is looking at what Chinese children are doing while at school. A significant amount of time in the Chinese school day is spent writing characters and memorizing stories. They rarely have projects and papers, but instead are told to work on things that require rote memory. Even a pre-school coloring book is filled with tracing paper so that everybody's apple will look exactly the same. Our kids come home with poems and stories to memorize every night. Well, that takes time. Lots of time. And that is why the Chinese system requires so many extra hours.

Their teaching tactics are also vastly different than the American system. For example, this week my five-year-old daughter has been reporting to me that her teachers have resorted to fear mongering to get the kids to bring their books to school. The teachers have threatened to cut the kids hair if they forget to bring their books. One child repeatedly forgot so one teacher took him behind a closed curtain and threatened to cut his hair. While he screamed, all the other five-year-olds were scared into silence. The teacher never actually cut his hair, but the little game was effective in motivating the kids to bring their books next time. The next day, someone broke a toy. The teacher asked for a confession from a class of kindergarteners and shockingly didn't get one child to raise their hands and admit guilt. It was at this point that she said she was going to look at surveillance cameras, find out, and then cut that child's shirt. Again, no surveillance cameras and no cutting of the shirt. My kids have been told by their teachers that I wouldn't pick them up from school until their lunch was eaten and that if they touched a bee, they would die.

The list of threats is long and extensive and has afforded us some great family discussions about authority. To most Americans, this looks manipulative and abusive. To the average Chinese, this is normal. You are to obey authority without question. They are taught that to stick out is to get hurt. "The gun kills the bird who leaves the nest first," is a common idiom to remind them that to jump too soon or make people notice you will only bring bad things your way. Listening to your teachers and obeying authorities makes you a good person. You do it without question. In living here for almost 7 years, I have almost never heard a Chinese child ask the question "Why?" They simply listen, memorize, and obey. If you saw the opening ceremonies of the Beijing Olympics in 2008, you will understand what I am talking about. It was one big mass of people all moving about as an extension of each other.

When a child gets something wrong, they are told they are dumb and next time they should be like Johnny Wang that sits next to him. This criticism is meant to motivate the child into perfection. You see, in a population of 1.4 billion people, perfection is the only dividing line. I used to get really worked up about how they educated their children, thinking it mean and excessive. From the Chinese perspective, it's loving and appropriate. To love your child or your student, you teach them to obey authority, wear warm clothing, and try your hardest in school. In her book, Amy Chua goes on to say that, "Chinese parents demand perfect grades because they believe that their child can get them. If their child doesn't get them, the Chinese parent assumes it's because the child didn't work hard enough." The longer I have lived here, the more I have come to appreciate the educational differences.

In the States, we are so concerned with the feelings of children that we are scared to make hard decisions for them. We are afraid that if we tell our children they aren't measuring up in school, they will curl into a low self-esteem glob of nothingness. As Americans, we get so overly concerned with making sure our children are our friends that we compromise in training them to become proper adults, not just our buddies.

Amy Chua outlines three main differences between the more Western style of parenting and the Chinese ways of raising children:

"First, I've noticed that Western parents are extremely anxious about their children's self-esteem…Chinese parents aren't. They assume strength, not fragility, and as a result they behave very differently.

Second, Chinese parents believe that their kids owe them everything.

Third, Chinese parents believe that they know what is best for their children and therefore override all of their children's own desires and preferences."

When you unpackage these three things, you take a sharp turn in comparing Western and Eastern parenting. With those three things as your premise, even getting up in the morning looks different.

There is a middle ground in here somewhere. A place where our kids understand that their actions have consequences. That when they fail at school, they are failing us as parents and failing themselves as future adults. I've come to appreciate that one of the most loving things a Chinese parent can do for their child is make sure they are healthy and succeed in school. Sometimes love is very practical. Maybe it's not the mushy kind of love I am used to, but it's love nonetheless.

I wrote the following blog the week the article came out and appropriately so, our inbox became flooded with questions about Chinese education.

## chinese mothering (blog: january 16, 2011)

There are basically two things that you have to decide upon as you settle into a parenting philosophy.

1. *What is my definition of "love?"*
   John Piper puts it beautifully by saying this:
   "The love of God is not God's making much of us, but God's saving us from self-centeredness so that we can enjoy making much of him forever. And our love to others is not our making much of them, but helping them to find satisfaction in making much of God. True love aims at satisfying people in the glory of God. Any love that terminates on man is eventually destructive. It does not lead people to the only lasting joy, namely, God. Love must be God-centered, or it is not true love; it leaves people without their final hope of joy."

As an American parent, our default setting is to love our children by making them happy. Chinese parents love their children by making sure they study hard and don't get sick. They love their children by assuring that they will have opportunities in the future.

We need to ask a few questions as we decide how we want to love our children:

What does it mean to express love to our kids? Some will hug and kiss them or tell them to wear a warmer coat. Others might work long hours, making enough money to send them to a good college.

What does it mean to receive love back from them? Many parents want to hear the words "I love you." Others will want to know they will be taken care of by their kids after retirement. Or that their kids will work hard to get good grades, therefore giving the family a good reputation.

In my day-to-day, what does love look like practically as I parent? For example, if I want my child to be a spelling bee champion, then five minutes after waking up we will throw toast on the table and start reviewing words. In contrast, if I want my children to learn to be a serve others and be generous, I need to have them bring meals for people and give their own toys away. Our goals for our children impact even the most minute decisions, like breakfast.

2.   *What kind of child do I want at age 18?*

At all the home school conferences I go to they encourage us to do a little self-reflection. We make a list of about 10 things that we want for our kids by the time they turn 18.

For example, we want our kids:

a. To love serving others.
b. To be able to share the gospel clearly with others.
c. To have a curiosity that spurs on their love for learning.
d. To have a global awareness.
e. To understand how to put together a logical argument.

These are just a few of ours. If my goal for my children was to have them be the top mathematician in their school, then I would start at five years old and drill them incessantly in math facts. By 12, they would understand algebra and spend many hours a day working out problems. This is where the Chinese parents flourish. They see the end goal, and they discipline their children to achieve that goal. Whether you agree with it or not, it is commendable that they stay the course. When their children whine and complain about not liking math, the Chinese parents don't waiver. Some might see this as excessive, but Chinese parents see it as incredibly loving. It all depends on how you define love and what you wish to see your children grow up to become.

In my opinion, the wisdom in the article comes when we step back and question our assumptions. Let us not be parents who just survive until the kids turn 18. Set vision. Stay the course. And pray like there's no tomorrow.

## just not cute anymore

Last night, we attended a little birthday shindig at a friend's house. I was casually chatting with another woman about world politics, the global economy, or maybe it was how much I love the waffle fries at Chic-Fil-A. I forget. I'm sure it wasn't the latter; I'm just far too sophisticated to talk about how I crave Chic-Fil-A fries every stinking SUNDAY that I'm in America!

Well, as we were discussing the finer points of whatever it was, my friend noticed my 2-year old daughter had her face crammed into her plate and was eating her food as if her mouth had been relocated to her forehead. We both laughed, but then I started thinking. Why is that no longer cute? I mean, as a grown adult, I could never get away with snorting my chocolate cake. I thought of a few more things that are so cute as a child that become unacceptable at some nebulous time right before puberty. For instance, fat thighs. Watching those things jiggle like a waterbed causes people to pull out their video cameras and capture the toddler's moment of glory. If I ran around in my skivvies and allowed my unmentionables to jiggle around, the only videotaping would be to mock me in front of a large YouTube audience.

What about eating spaghetti with your hands? I don't know of a family in America that doesn't have at least one good "spaghetti all over the kid" picture. When I eat spaghetti and the noodle whips my upper lip, splattering red sauce up my nose, people laugh, but not because it's cute. They are laughing at me…clearly not with me because I'm not laughing.

The final one that came to mind was the Buddha gut. That cute stage where a sizable roll of fat lops itself over their pants. We grab it, jiggle it, and rub it for good luck. This same gut 25 years later causes us to invent things like Spandex. And to wear said Spandex even if it causes profuse sweating and constriction of our lungs, because we WILL still fit into those trendy jeans from college. Oh how I miss the freedoms and lack of public concern that kids seem to possess.

## transforming a gigolo

Truly believing that he was a Transformer, Corbin made up a way to say "You want a piece of me!" in Chinese. Our friend said that technically it's accurate, but it's not the way they would say it. "But," she said, "you can say it that way inside your house." As Corbin plowed through the house chanting his new phrase, a tower of confidence began to build in his lanky little body. We invited that same Chinese friend to come with us out to dinner one night, and Corbin decided to test out whether or not his new Chinese trash talk would provoke fear in the waitress. He looked at her with curved eyebrows and a subtle head nod to tell her, "You want a piece of me?!" Shocked, the waitress laughed and quickly bused our table. As she walked uncomfortably away with an armload of dishes, we turned to look at our friend. At that same moment, our friend was shaking her head that was buried deep in her hands. She went on to explain that the reason she told him it was an in-house phrase only was because that it actually meant, "Are you sexually attracted to me?"

## my husband's adoption conversion

We have always been advocates for the idea of adoption. For years, we waved the banner for the cause and told other people that it was a great plan for their lives. Adoption had been something we considered on several occasions and something that I would secretly research while my husband was away on business. It felt like some secret escapade that I would reveal to him after the fact. He graciously let me rattle on and on about some child on a waiting list in Haiti or an Indonesian island pummeled by an earthquake leaving dozens of children without caretakers. He felt my concern but he seemed to keep it at an arms length from his heart. Distance can keep you safe, but it can also leave you left out.

We were living up in Northern China when a little girl named Yue Yue pulled the drawstrings on the distance between idea and reality for him regarding adoption. Our friend Liu Ayi had been a nanny for several children over the last 25 years. For about nine months, she cared for Grace like she was her own. I was in language school at the time and Liu Ayi would take Grace outside to catch butterflies, eat green pea ice cream and tell her a Chinese word over and over, hoping to reach the 10,000 times she said it took for a child to learn a new word. All the frolicking and blissful days came to a screeching halt when she decided that Grace was hot and proceeded to cut her hair. Grace came home with a jagged pixie cut that very aptly described the chaos of cultural conflict that would ensue over the next 24 hours.

With the amount of Chinese we knew at the time, ordering dinner and sending a letter was about all we were good for. Our friend acted as a translator and explained to Liu Ayi that you can't just decide to chop off our one-year-old's hair without first consulting us. Weaving through the gates of culture, we found ourselves at the other end frustrated and tired. She quit. The loss of face that she had incurred because we had to get a translator to communicate with her and the fact that we had our friend call her back that night to make sure she understood, was just too much; she had lost face to strangers and was told she was wrong by people younger than her. But we remained friends with her and would see her casually on the street buying cabbage and sweet potatoes.

A few months later we got word that Liu Ayi had suffered a small stroke and was declining in health. Thankfully, she recovered, but still found herself sluggish and tired throughout the day. Too add to her difficulties, her relationship with her daughter was broken and her husband worked long hours at a clothing factory. One morning, there was a knock at her door. As she pulled herself to the door, she was shocked to see a sullen little girl and her disheveled young mother. The mother was looking at Liu Ayi as if she knew why she was standing outside a stranger's house, but not quite sure she wanted to retrace the steps had brought got her there.

Bright black hair, an uncomfortably short skirt that had taken her unmentionable places and a daughter gripping her mother's hand as she dealt with the inevitable. Whether it was a smoky corner in a nightclub or sitting in a cold chair at the back of a pool hall, this little girl was familiar with such scenes. Her wandering mother had visions of reading bedtime stories to fill her little girl's ears with hope and comfort, but the voices of money and men were so persistent that she could no longer scream loud enough to drown them out. The voices had preached her a convincing message. A message that told her to abandon the things that hold you down and turn your days into burden.

For now, that very thing was a child. The child that she dreamed would become a ballerina or an astronaut while she was inside of her. The little girl who grabbed her mother's hand while jumping off the second step for the first time. The same daughter that patted her mother's arm asking for breakfast while her mother was passed out from the night before.

This young mother now found herself on the doorstep of a stranger asking for part of her to be taken away. She told Liu Ayi that she was following her boyfriend's lead and traveling around the country. There was no scheduled day of return nor a purpose for her departure. The voices in her head merely told her this was a good idea. The woman was giving her daughter away to a stranger. Shyly, the little girl shuffled into Liu Ayi's home and stood in the corner with her hands politely folded in front of her. She put her head down and said nothing for the next 12 hours. This was a routine well practiced.

Liu Ayi peeled oranges and handed them to the silent little girl. She washed the dirt from her cheeks and pulled on warm socks in the morning, just as she had done with Grace. Yue Yue brought new life to Liu Ayi's day and the little girl's light began to dimly return to her eyes. She still didn't speak much and she found comfort in her fear for a better part of the day. With Liu Ayi's health and financial situation both in shambles, we began to get practical. The kids and I rounded up toys, clothes, snacks and blankets to bring to Yue Yue. Jackson and I spent late nights talking about if the situation arose, could we adopt her; would we adopt her? As Jackson looked into this little girl's lost eyes, he saw adoption for the first time. The tug of that little girl's hand pulled adoption off of a page and fashioned it into a little girl. From that day forward, adoption became more than just curious research, it became the pursuit of a child.

That's the funny thing about adoption-until there is a realization that adoption is not so much about rescuing an orphan as it is bringing home a child and understanding the gospel in it all, you can keep it at the level of "a nice thing to do." And then the Lord drops an orphan into your life who looks at you and hopes, even if it's just for a second that they could be the one you read to at night before being tucked in. It's for these children that we pursue adoption. It's for these children that we continue to advocate. It's these children that remind me of my utter desperation and lostness I found myself wrapped up in before Christ came in and folded me into His child.

A few months later, Yue Yue's mother came stumbling back into the picture. She came by unannounced one day to reclaim her daughter as if she was a package forgotten at the post office. While this little girl's story will probably not have a happy ending, the sentences of her story that intersected with ours have changed our lives forever.

## *giving birth in a foreign country*

My fourth child, Levi was born in Thailand. He still enjoys telling people that he is Thai even with his white skin and American passport. After you have lived overseas for some time, you learn to be really flexible and just kind of roll with unfamiliar situations. Birthing in Thailand was a new one for me. I arrived in Thailand in a very fat, very pregnant state. I only had a couple of weeks until my due date, so we had to figure out the doctor thing quickly and get ready for birth #4.

Upon entering the hospital to find a doctor, the nurse asked me a very simple question, "Do you want a natural birth?" But, mind you, with that question came a very thick Thai accent. To my American ears, the question was, "Do you want a national bird?" Immediately, my thoughts were, "Oh how fun! It's like Hawaii when you get off the plane and they put a bright flower lei around your neck, welcoming you to their home." I guess when you give birth in Thailand, they send you home with a national bird. I had visions of my new baby in one arm and a large wooden cage with a magpie in the other.

I glanced over to Jackson and then back at the lady and asked her to repeat her question. Again, I heard "Do you want a national bird?" I shrugged my shoulders, trying to be culturally sensitive and not make strange faces at this bizarre custom. "Sure!" I replied with much enthusiasm. Thinking my response was filled with a little too much gusto for the question that the nurse actually asked, Jackson grabbed my arm and asked if I understood what she was saying to me. "Yes, I understand. She wants to know if I want a national bird? Isn't that cool that they do that here?!"

Rolling his eyes, he told the nurse to take me back to the natural birthing area and explained to me what had actually happened. It wasn't a national bird, but a natural birth that the nurse was asking me about. I still think it would be fabulous to get a national bird after giving birth.

I ate fried rice every meal for a day and a half, watched 87 Jean-Claude Van Damme movies, and got asked by two different nurses why I was still fat. Apparently after giving birth, Thai women spring out of bed for an afternoon of tennis in their short mini skirts. Actually, lots of women over here put on a girdle type thing after giving birth. They want things to go back to normal quickly, so they believe that wearing a girdle hastens that. After one day, I went home with my newborn son…and no magpie.

In China, after you have a baby, you are in "baby prison" for 30 days. Your mom is supposed to come over and attend to your every need. And your needs at this time include eating only eggs and broth. Lots and lots of eggs. You are not to sit up, brush your hair, take a shower, or even roll over to watch TV. These activities will give you arthritis when you are older. You should only lay there and look at your baby for 30 days. I tell my friends that the day after giving birth to my first child, my mom helped me too. She helped me order a Starbucks after we walked to the mall. They cannot believe it and give me a stern "tsk tsk," because it is now fated to me that I will indeed have arthritis as a grown woman. I tell them that if I'm gonna go down, it will at least be with a coffee in hand. And again, the "tsk tsk."

## why girls matter

I was on the way out to pick up four of my kids from their morning at Chinese school yesterday when I ran into a new friend who lives on the fifth floor of our apartment building. We have just moved to our new city and I've literally been begging God for friends since we arrived. My instinct was to say hi and rush off to get my children. But, realizing that the Lord was answering my prayers, I stopped and asked her how things were going. After about 10 minutes of chatting, she began to tell me about her childhood. It's always so interesting when Chinese tell stories that are shameful to them. They start speaking softly, often laughing at uncomfortable places. They toss their eyes over their shoulders, looking around to make sure that nobody else is listening. The blessing in being a foreigner is that we are pseudo-disconnected from their circles of influence. We can listen with safe ears because we don't have mouths that will speak these hurtful things to others and therefore bring loss of face to our friends. It's a privileged position that we get to take.

Because of China's agricultural economy and the one child policy, many people have a twisted view of female children and their usefulness. I will say that this is changing, though. City people are much more embracing of having girls. Many families are finding that the girls actually do a better job of helping their aging parents later on. But there are still many in China, especially in the more rural areas, who think that girls are inferior to boys. There are lots of dynamics at play here, but mostly it's a pragmatic opinion. Boys can work hard in the fields or factories and help provide for their families. Culturally, after boys get married they will take care of their families, oftentimes living with their parents. If you have a little girl, she will grow up, get married, and go to live and care for her husband's family. When you put yourselves in their shoes, it all makes sense. To them, girls are not useful. When you are making $100 a month, sentimentality is a luxury that most just can't afford. I am thankful that this tide is changing in the cities, and it will eventually trickle into the rural areas.

So yesterday as I was talking to my fifth floor friend, she was explaining how these dynamics have directly affected her life. She has an older sister and an older brother (she was born before the one child policy took effect). When she came along, her mother was devastated. Her parents certainly didn't want another girl. This would only add another burden to the family. The family decided to get rid of her. Mercifully, they gave her to a grandparent in another city. They didn't want contact with her, but just to forget that her life had ever happened. Well, 4 or 5 years later, the grandparent gave her back. She didn't explain why, it just happened. She went on to tell me that her mother had another girl a few years later and proceeded to abandon her somewhere. "Maybe some nice foreigner like you guys adopted her!" was her hopeful response.

My friend has now become a mother of a 6-year old boy and a 15-month-old girl. I asked her if she wanted to do all she could to protect her little girl. "Yes, yes, yes!" she exclaimed, beaming in pride at her little girl's chance at life. Her parents and her in-laws advised her to get rid of her little girl days after she was born.

There are stories after stories of children tossed aside or haphazardly given to family members to raise. Once a child is abandoned, they have virtually no citizenship. The Chinese child only has a name and citizenship attached to their parents. Without a parent and a city to claim, it is nearly impossible to get an ID card. This ID card allows them to attend schools, get jobs, travel, and basically survive. Without this, life is hard. Unbearably hard.

Adoption to the Chinese mind is shameful and unheard of. If you do adopt a child, it's because you can't give birth naturally or you have some type of bad intentions for that child. Because of the one child policy, there is no space for adoption to be normalized.

Now…cut and paste our family onto this backdrop.

We can obviously birth children. Our family already had four children that share our blood, and to the Chinese mind that is a blessing. But then to adopt another child, born from another mother, from another country, and with skin the opposite color of ours is a staggering fact for them. It does not compute on so many levels. We get asked all the time if we are going to tell Joi that she is adopted. I tell them that of course we'll tell her because adoption is a blessing from the Lord. She is our gift and we will treasure her like we treasure and care for our other children. I'm also pretty sure she'll figure it out when she starts connecting the skin color dots.

I cannot tell you how many times I have been able to talk about Jesus and His adoption of me due to people's curiosity about our family. I tell them that I want to love others because Christ first loved us. Does our family make sense? No, but neither does the extravagance of the cross; neither does the mercy that I get shown each day I wake up and take a first breath; and neither does the fact that my sins have been lifted off my death sentence.

I am excited about my new friendship that the Lord has given me. She loves her daughter dearly and wants to see her flourish. There is nothing like watching a mother beam as she talks about her hopes for her children. I imagine this is the way the Lord must look at us: jealous for our allegiance fervent in His protection of our faith, and hopeful for our lives.

## *irreverent weddings with relevant ceremony*

We have attended lots of weddings here and find it fascinating at how they are conducted. While there is some variation, for the most part Chinese weddings all look very similar. Many of the couples go to a fortuneteller-type person to find out their lucky day and time. You will see weddings happening at 9 am on a Tuesday morning. Claiming a non-religious culture, no day is considered sacred. Tuesday seems just as arbitrary as a Saturday or Sunday. The morning of the wedding is spent in preparation. Much like a Western wedding, the bride gets her hair done while the groom spends time with family and friends that are frantically running around sticking flowers and signs everywhere. Oftentimes, the friends and family will go around the house or apartment complex looking for drain holes and sewage covers to place a red symbol on top of. They are trying to prevent bad spirits from coming in and blessings from going out through any openings.

After the preparations are finished, the bride and groom play a kind of cat and mouse game. At our friend's wedding, we were honored by getting to attend this more personal part of the ceremony. This is the same friend that lovingly put down the blue saucer for me to use as a bathroom in the middle of the night. First, the groom goes into a bedroom to hide a pair of red shoes. Once they are hidden, all parties except for the bride and her brother or parents leave the room. The groom waits with his parents outside until they are told to enter the house again. The groom eventually heads back to the bedroom and knocks on the door of the bride. The brother talks through the door and proceeds to negotiate a dowry with the groom. As the poor groom offers money and precious material goods, the brother refuses until he feels like the price befits his sister's hand in marriage. The brother then reluctantly opens the door to allow the bride and groom to spend a couple of minutes together laughing and enjoying one another. I love that part. Things can be so formal for Chinese families that I love when they forget their decorum and just laugh.

At this point, everyone except the family is told to leave the room. We were privileged to sit with the family and eat some small snacky type things with them. It was so interesting glancing around that table. The groom's family were very poor farmers and the bride's were a retired teacher and a blue collar worker. None of the parents had much money. But to look at them beam with pride as they celebrated the wedding of their daughter who had earned a Master's degree and the son who was going to do PhD work in England was amazing. The parents had succeeded in giving their children a future that involved neither tending to harsh crops or slaving in the hot factories just to put rice in their bowls. They had also succeeded in getting their daughter married off before she turned 30. The bride, 27, barely made it. If she surpasses 30, she is considered a leftover and the family will begin to lose more and more face as each year passes. The unfortunate part of this is that you will see many believers settle with a non-believing spouse because they cannot bare the loss of face that remaining unmarried might bring to their families.

The bride and groom are expectant and nervous. There is so much going on at that small table and around those simple snacks. Because I was dear friends with the bride, I could read her face like a familiar novel. She was concerned about her future, excited that it was her wedding day, and yet skeptical that being married would change her state of happiness. Her husband is a wonderful man and treats her well. But after they got engaged, he reminded her that one day he would probably find a mistress. As his career got going, finding a more interesting woman would be a part of being successful. My friend knew this going into marriage. She hated it, but she saw no other option. She was quickly approaching 30 and she would rather be replaced than rejected.

But on that wedding day she did seem happy. Maybe just relieved.

As the wedding progressed, we headed to the restaurant. Because this is officially an atheistic country, weddings have become a rather irreverent affair. When we first moved here, this would drive me crazy. But, as I processed it more and more, I realized there was no reason for me to expect anything else. Instead I should be bothered when unbelievers confess allegiance to God, Christ, and each other solely because they are getting married in a church. At least my Chinese non-believing friends weren't trying to fake a belief. The couple rents out a spacious section of a restaurant and sets up large tables for the guests to sit and attend the ceremony. Similar to their dreams for the future, they fill every empty shadow with customarily appropriate items. The bulky tables spot the room. Lanky bottles of beer cascade over the glass table, reflecting a skyline of modernity and sophistication. Before the party begins, the couple drives up in a rented car dressed in carnations and pink chiffon. When they step out of the car, they are showered in silly string, confetti, and an explosion of fireworks.

All the guests head upstairs and take a seat at a round table. At the table there are usually large serving platters of cigarettes, small snacks, and bottles of juice, coke and beer. At this particular ceremony, two of my children were asked to be the flower girl and ring bearer. This happens often because people love the idea of having little blonde foreign kids as a centerpiece on their wedding day. Just two weeks ago a lady came up to me wanting our kids to be in their wedding. I had never met these people. They were going to buy dresses and have this whole production where my kids would be dressed as angels and do some kind of performance during her son's wedding. I graciously declined.

As I was standing in the back, wrangling my two wedding performers, I looked to send them on their way. Except there were no aisles or rings. My daughter held a basket and threw flowers while dodging the dinner tables and my son carried an empty pillow. They bobbed and weaved through the chairs and guests looking like Heisman contenders. Once they made it to the front, I grabbed them both to sit down in the front.

My husband was asked to be the officiator of the wedding, which also meant that he would give a brief message on marriage. This was a big blessing, as the entire room was filled with non-believers. It would have been an even bigger blessing had anybody actually listened. At that point, neither of us could speak Chinese, so he used a translator to share his message. We prayed afterwards that the words he said to the translator would land on a fertile heart. She was probably the only person who could hear what he was saying. All the other guests were simultaneously digging into the beer and cigarettes while laughing in unison. Towards the end of the ceremony, the bride gives her new parents a flower. Sometimes the groom will do the same. This is symbolizing to the in-laws that they have just been granted a new son or daughter. Each will be expected to call them Mom and Dad from that day forward.

The bride usually changes a couple of times during this restaurant ceremony. Nowadays, the girl will rent a white Western style dress for the first part of the ceremony and change into a more traditional red dress later on in the evening. Under her white dress is the pair of red shoes that she found in the room earlier on in the day. As a side note, it totally makes more sense to rent a bridal dress. What a waste of money to buy one. Mine is sitting in some box somewhere. That is one expensive storage item.

At our friend's wedding, Jackson wrapped things up from the "pulpit" and the food rolled out in waves. If there is not enough food for all the guests, the family will be shamed among their community. To prevent this generational disgrace, they over order. And by over ordering I mean 30 dishes for a table of six. We have at least 10 dishes that go completely untouched by anyone at our table.

After the festivities are over, people stumbled out onto the sidewalks to head home. Weddings are a smoky, loud, chaotic affair, but I have learned to overlook the obvious irreverence while enjoying being able to celebrate with our friends. We have felt so honored getting to celebrate with friends by attending their weddings and squirting silly string on unsuspecting brides. It's different than what I am used to in the States, but it is still a treasure, cigarette platters and all.

### the day i dreamt about adoption paperwork

We decided to adopt from Ethiopia the week before the stock market plummeted in the US in 2008. This was our confirmation that we didn't dream up this little scheme ourselves. God would have to be the one to lead us through those deep, narrow woods. While international adoption is hard anywhere, add the extra layer of being an American, living in China, adopting from Ethiopia, and it makes you want to poke yourself in the eye with a toothpick. But since the Lord often calls our family to do things the hard way, we made the phone calls to agencies to try and find one that would work with us and our unique circumstances.

One of the biggest hurdles was the time difference between where we lived and America. China doesn't do time zones, so depending on the season, we would be 13 or 14 hours ahead of our adoption agency. The lack of time zones also give my children the idea that because the sun comes up at 4 a.m., it is also time to wake up and ask for breakfast. Both of these time zone issues have gone badly for us. My husband and I spent many nights with our alarm set for 1:30 a.m. so that we could wake up and do a conference call with our agency in the States.

We also got into the habit of rushing to our emails once we woke up to check on the status of things. If we didn't, the workday in the States would end and we would have to wait an entire 24 hours for a response to a question we had. This scheduling added to my neurotic tendencies. One day, I was frustrated at the lag time in getting emails, so I Facebook stalked our social worker Sharon, who lived in Texas. I knew that if she was posting a comment on Facebook, that her internet was working and she had read (and should be promptly responding) to my emails. My husband told me I was obsessive and needed professional help. I though stalking her on Facebook was a genius plan.

That weekend, after I Facebook accosted our social worker, we headed to Beijing. Our family was on its way to Thailand for a conference and maybe a cheap massage, but had several adoption things to do in Beijing before we could head out. We spent the first day mingling with lovely embassy employees and finishing up the adoption paperwork that we were frantically trying to finish before we left the country. At one point our social worker's email was down, and then our email went down. The only way we could communicate with her was through Facebook. These were questions that needed fast answers or else we would have missed deadlines. My stalking paid off. I walked the rest of the day with a strut of self-vindication.

We jumped the embassy hurdles and now needed to find a place that would mail our documents to Texas. The documents we needed to mail included months of late night phone calls, trips to the smoky Chinese police stations, tears of waiting, and hundreds of dollars spent getting things stamped. I felt like we were putting Moses in his basket to be shipped down the Nile. Because our mail is frequently picked-through before we receive it, we wanted to use an international mail carrier that we recognized. UPS's address came up on Google maps, so we tore off to catch them before the office closed for the day. The cold bit through our jackets and the wind whipped at us from behind, but at last we had arrived in the shadows of our beloved UPS building. It was as if we had fought our way through the elements up to the summit of Mount Everest. We all ran inside so we could untangle ourselves and defrost our appendages.

We pushed floor 16 and started to wonder what kind of UPS office we were headed towards. But there was no time for rational thinking, the documents had to be mailed off immediately. We clicked through the marble floor hallways and swung open the glass doors to be greeted by a pleasantly perplexed secretary. While I spent the next 2 hours playing soccer with my 4 kids out in the hallway, Jackson spent the time meticulously copying the documents. The secretary lady showed him the closet room with the copier, and he copied a solid 200 pages. As he looked around, there were cubicles and dress ties. This was not a UPS mailing station, this was UPS corporate in Beijing. Probably the headquarters for all of China, or by the looks of things, the entire Eastern Hemisphere. Upon realizing this, he continued to play the dumb foreigner card and not only proceeded to make copies, but also asked for post it notes, a stapler, folders and a few envelopes.

I offered my children as a decoy a few times to distract them from the complete inappropriateness of us being in their office trying to mail something. He finished his copying, got everything into the envelope, and then she pretended to punch on her calculator what it would cost to mail this thing to Texas. We paid her and ran out the door as if we had just been caught in the opposite-gender's bathroom. But it worked, and we walked out the door with candy and several pieces of UPS Beijing Olympic sponsorship paraphernalia. One of the things we have learned over here is that you can get away with things as a foreigner, especially if you have little children, that nobody else can. And so…we do.

We crashed into our beds at our crowded hostel to prepare for travel the next morning. Before going to bed, we emailed our social worker and told her to expect our precious Moses package to arrive at her office Monday morning. Like Pavlovian dogs, we woke up the next morning twitching to check email, just because. We didn't expect anything pressing, but felt the urge. Our adoption referral wouldn't be for at least three months, so I'm not even sure what we were so eager for. As we scrolled through the Lowe's ads and emails promising a cheap time-share in the Caribbean, we saw an email from Sharon. Figuring it was just a confirmation that she received our email, I continued to change diapers on the floor and fold the sheets to conspicuously hide the creamed carrots that had stained the corner. Jackson gasped and turned around to tell me that we had received a referral for a 6-month-old little girl. 10 hours after sending our paperwork in the mail. Not three months, not even an entire lunar cycle. We were both in shock and I went on to memorize every shadow in that picture so I could think about that little girl while we traveled. We later found out that the exact same day that we mailed off our documents in Beijing, her birth mother was making the hardest decision of her life. It was the day that she would drop Joi off at an orphanage in hopes that a family would come and make her their own.

Our paperwork that was sent to Sharon started a chain reaction that would eventually get us the forms we would need to travel and get our daughter. Our paperwork was now sitting at homeland security waiting to be approved for our next step. We waited and waited. There were phone calls to the embassy, emails to homeland security and scanned documents galore, but never a response that our paperwork was being tended to. Three slow months later, our forms had still not been reviewed. My non-patience was setting in. We could not do anything until these forms were reviewed and the next set sent to us to fill out and return. At about this point, I had to resort to Nyquil to get my anxious muscles to relax enough to sleep.

One night though, I had a dream. The dream was vivid and poignant. In the dream, a voice said to me, "Your paperwork is not being taken care of. It's sitting on a desk." No gleaming angels or bushes on fire, a simple statement from the Lord. One of the graces that has been given to me is dreams. They happen a few times a year and every time, I know it's the Lord. I just know. Like when you knew the person you were marrying was "the one." I woke up the next morning and told Jackson that we had to call the embassy at 8:30 am. He was skeptical because this office had not answered their phones in over five weeks. I called and a man named James picked up the phone. He told me that my paperwork wasn't being taken care of and that it was just sitting on a person's desk. I told him I know this and then shared my dream. I'm sure he thought I had lost it and went on to track my call and put me on a no-fly list. He said he was very sorry for the mix-up and that he would have my forms sent out in a week. I thanked him a dozen times and offered to name my next child after him. I emailed him our address and asked for his supervisor's name so that I could put in a good word for him. He took our address and never responded about the supervisor thing. When we got the documents that week, they were all signed and stamped by the Field Supervisor, James. The boss man had been the one to answer my phone call that day. The boss man that probably has 8 different secretaries and many more important things to do like stop global terrorism. That same man cleared the way for us to find our baby girl.

### adoption ditty

No, I cannot sing.
No, it has no music.

But I wanted to write a song about the transformation we experienced while trudging through the adoption process. It's written from the perspective of me speaking to Joi and from Jesus speaking to His children.

As I wrote it, I wanted to convey how I felt as we went through the process to get Joi. Nightly, I would look at her picture and yearn for her to know that we were coming. I would face her picture that sat on my computer and tell her "Good night, baby, we are coming!" I cried myself to sleep more than once as I turned away from her and tried to muster enough peace to fall asleep. The computer-framed picture was the only thing I had that gave me hope that all the red tape would someday turn into a daughter. During that process, I understood the longing Jesus has for His children. We wander and foutter along, having no idea that Jesus is caring for us-that He is waiting for the day when we call Him Father. He looks at our "frame" (Ps. 139) and lovingly counts the hairs on our heads. So this little ditty is two-fold. Hopefully it conveys my thoughts about wanting Joi as my daughter and wanting to yell through the computer screen "I am coming. Just wait! I'm here!" It also shares how Jesus longs for His children's hearts, for their trust. He so desperately wants His children to understand that His hand is secure; that He is there and won't abandon them. I want Joi to get that. Jesus wants *us* to get that.

## I am Here

I stare at your frame thinking of your future,
but wanting your today.
Believe in my presence, look for my grace.

There will be a time when close won't seem so far
When you will trust in my voice as the moon does the stars.

There will be a day when you will find no season to blame
'cause I have breathed life into your heart.
I have given you a new name.

I need you to know I am not leaving.
I need you to know I am here to stay.
Till dawn breaks new mercies
Till waking brings new days.
I am here.

I cover your future, grace covers today.
Grip onto my promise that redemption's been made.
Rest my child, you don't have to try
I carry your freedom, I've given you life

I am not leaving, you belong to me
in the dark of the night, hope as you dream.
For I am counting your days, measuring your time.
'til I can clean off your hurts
and say "You are mine."

I need you to know I am not leaving.
I need you to know I am here to stay.
Till dawn breaks new mercies
Till waking brings new days.
I am here.

I wish I could restore days lost to wondering
if I existed, if anyone was coming.
But child, I am here now and tomorrow the same.
For when I look down, I see not an orphan
but a child wearing my name.

I need you to know I am not leaving.
I need you to know I am here to stay.
Till dawn breaks new mercies
Till waking brings new days.
I am here.

## in the shadows

As I sit here, my husband is at a very important meeting and I am at home with my kids. This is a relatively normal day for me. It's in these moments that the vines of being needed creep up and suffocate the hope and purpose from my soul. I look at the work he is getting to do and I allow self-pity and loathing to replace any sort of joy I should be getting. It can be so easy sometimes to forget that I have purpose in each day. Sometimes that purpose is to remain joyful while I plow through dishes. Other times it is to open my mouth to talk about Jesus with street vendors. But honestly, one feels more valiant than the other.

I cannot loathe the daily because the daily is what makes up a week, followed by a month. After I look back at that month, I should see small victories. I should rejoice at being quick to listen and slow to speak. I should relish the hug from the girl at the orphanage that has refused to make eye contact for the last three months. When I define 'eternal things' with my own words, I miss God in the daily things. I have found that it's usually in these small things that God gives us a spectacle of the ordinary. He displays Himself in my heart as showing financial grace to a beggar and finding joy in doing laundry. That is a true miracle and is the workmanship of His hands alone. It's in these times of feeling like a shadow that I remember that it's those very shadows that allow a fire to dance. Both the obvious fire and the subtle shadows have to exist together or we would simply be sitting around a pile of hot ash.

I love when God gives us an overwhelming sense of who He is. I cannot imagine that day when I stand before Him in all His glory. That 15 minutes of insight was almost more than my soul could take. Thank you Lord for small glimpses and large graces.

# Life Over Here

"I sought the Lord, and he answered me and
delivered me from all my fears."

Psalms 34:4 (ESV)

*Even though we have been over here for most of my children's lives, we are always surprised by how much we learn about this place we call home. But now the people, festivals, foods, and sounds have been lifted from a tour guide and into the photo album of our family life.*

## Kite Flying

At the end of spring, one of the traditions that I love here is kite flying. A lot of people will undertake the task of making a homemade kite. I prefer to support the local economy by just buying one. I'm sure it has nothing to do with my being a complete imbecile when it comes to constructing things.

The old men have these kites crafted together with 15-foot tails and string half a mile long. They have learned how to make these kites dance. All these men start the kites out without running. The liftoff is the most humiliating part of kite flying. You run like you're being chased by a bank robber and all the while your kite is skipping along behind you. It's not catching any wind, it's just making you run harder in hopes of it stumbling upon a pocket of air. As I'm running like a crazy lady being chased by a python, the old men just stand there flirting their kites into the air like a Jedi. And they are laughing at me, my running, and the kite that's playing leapfrog with the ground. Every time we go out to fly kites, there is an old man in a wheel chair with his kite up near federal aviation territory. He gets special delight in my failed attempts to succeed at a toy made for an 8-year old.

Before the kids are ready to take on the feat of flying a kite, they practice on unsuspecting bugs. During the spring, dragon flies twitter about and fly close to the ground. Our kids and their friends will catch them and tie a string around the bug's abdomen. Then they fly them…like a kite. I'm pretty sure the dragonflies die after awhile, but I do get a little thrill out of watching a playground full of children flying their bugs.

*star-studded performance*

There are times when you know that an event is blog-worthy, so you bring your camera and you think up witty one-liners as the event is happening. This afternoon was one such occasion. The Chinese love to put on performances. There doesn't really need to be the excuse of a holiday or celebration to perform. They just do it. And they do it with much vigor.

This little doozy of a performance happened right in our apartment complex this afternoon. One guy kicked things off with a riveting song and dance routine. At one point he leapt off the stage, danced around, and then sang to an empty car. As I look around, I counted sixty-three people in the audience. But to him, it was a sold out concert in Central Park. In my opinion, that made it even funnier to watch.

Next up was this adorable grandma-soldier-wonder woman routine. All 72 years of her marched around and shot an air gun...many, many times. I have to admit, I was brainstorming all the things I could do with those Wonder Woman leggings. They would sure add some pep to my home schooling routine.

When an older lady performs, usually it's her personal rendition of Beijing Opera. I know that this is a cultural gem here, but honestly it sounds like what you would hear if there was a wild cat who is being swung around really fast...by its tail... while in heat. And at least the cats have something potentially good that could come from being in heat. There is no such possible good in hearing Beijing Opera. But the older people in the audience were on the brink of lighting their lighters, swaying back and forth, and singing "Free Bird."

The entertainment only got better when I saw who was up next. This guy started by gliding his feet in a familiar fashion. Within the first 10 seconds, I realized that he must have watched Michael Jackson's "Bad" video eighty-three times in order to memorize not only the moves but also the facial expressions. When I say that his performance made me happy, that is a gross understatement. I looked and looked around for my only American friend that lives near us, but she was not to be found. I desperately needed someone to experience this with me.

But alas, I was alone, laughing so hard I was crying. And to top it off, the wind was blowing, so this guy's white over shirt was blowing behind him, just like Michael's did. It was pure delight. The climax of the performance was when he was running in place. Running with passion, zeal, and speed. I think he stole this move from "Footloose." I couldn't blame the guy... it's a classic move.

As a side note, I just re-lived this routine while I was writing. I now have cramps and tears dripping down my face. This routine will be my new happy place for the week.

As he ended his song, he rushed to the front of the stage and reached out to grab a few hands of his adoring fans.

Happy place. Happy, happy place.

### *dressing according to dates*

It is officially hot now. We have surpassed the elusive spring where there is an occasional cool day. Every year at this time, we get more and more criticism about how we dress our children. The Chinese dress according to dates. June 15th, the air-conditioning will turn on and people will be allowed to wear shorts. It's the end of April and around 80 degrees Fahrenheit here now, yet people are still in long underwear and jackets. I've even had friends tell me that they were so hot, but they just couldn't bare the idea of taking off their long underwear. They will sweat and tire but still refuse to dress according to the weather. Our Chinese friends even tell us that all our kids will get sick if they continue this irresponsible way of dressing each morning. But to allow their kids to wear shorts before June 15th would be an unforgivable sin to the grandparents and a cultural mishap on so many levels. At least once a week, my children come home from Chinese school with some other kid's clothing on. The teachers claim that either my children are uncomfortable or cold, so they gave them something else to wear.

When I was pregnant with #4, I got in trouble all the time for dressing in the wrong clothes, sitting on the cold floor and therefore losing my calcium, eating things other than broth with chicken bones, and not resting all day while my mother tended to my other children. We would patiently explain that our cultures were different. I'm not even sure my mom would want to move in with us! I also explained that if we were hot, then we would wear lighter clothing. This makes no sense to them. It's at these moments that I have to remember that we were all conditioned by our own cultures. There are things we do and say that we just can't release. The idea of wearing shorts before June 15th is just one of those things here.

## My Little Garden

Garden Oh Garden, I planted you so
I could be organic as I watch you grow.

The idea of eating straight from the earth
Sounds ideal but I'm not sure it's worth

The watering and prepping I'm having to do
The work that is needed to make it through.

I prefer to let God tend to all of your needs,
To provide water and sun for your little seeds.

And when you slump and when you die
I can blame it on the rain, the sun and the sky.

## Chinese picture taking

There is much to be learned culturally by how Chinese take pictures. Here's the scene:

There is an ominous pagoda outlined in popping pink cherry blossoms. Leaning against a fake rock in black orthopedics and navy blue oversized trousers is a Chinese man. The pants are fastened securely three inches above his belly button shifting his pants three long inches above his white athletic socks. His hands are tipped to the right and are positioned in a "V." Every time, the "V." This connotes victory. Over what, we're not sure, but victory nonetheless. If the subject is a male, then there is no smile. Only a serious posture as if he is sitting in on a meeting with the UN on nuclear proliferation. If the subject is female, there is a subtle smile as if they have just been told by their mothers to grin and say thank you for the socks Grandma gave them for Christmas. In the other hand is a flower. This flower is placed right along her cheekbone. The camera is always at least 15 feet away from the subject. The point is for the people to blend into the background. The scenery is just as important as the person in it. The pictures are brushed with all types of background with very little space reserved for a person.

The opposite is true of our American pictures. We zoom in as close as possible to our subjects, even cutting off a hairline or dimpled chin. The faces should be poured into the pictures, leaving very little room for fake rocks, dusty pagodas or daisies lining our jawbones. We don't want to blend into the background. That would imply that we aren't the focal point of the picture.

This leisurly activity becomes cultural commentary as you look at how each subject is viewed. The Chinese see themselves as a small part of a larger whole. We Americans want to be a large part of a smaller whole. The individual is first. To be unique is to win. The Chinese think that there is more identity to be had when they are defined as a group. We Americans only like to identify ourselves with a group when our group is winning. I am always a Houston Astros fan until October when play-offs roll around. Come October, I abandon ship and throw on my Boston Red Sox hat. At that point, relating to the Red Sox is much more fun.

Both perspectives are important to understand and embrace. As an American, I need to learn to step back and allow those around me to be pulled up to the foreground. I need to allow my person to be watermarked into my surroundings every once in awhile. To greater increase the beauty of things and people normally overlooked.

## *thailand rest*

Whenever we travel to Thailand, we feel as if a heavy woolen blanket has been lifted from our bodies and replaced with a soft, silky sheet. While I love living in China, there is also a certain amount of stress that is a constant companion while living overseas. You find yourself needing more sleep, eating more, getting easily overwhelmed, and even agitated at simple life tasks. China is loud. Horns are in a permanent state of honking, and the language sounds sharp and abrasive, like two old ladies fighting over the last package of pimento loaf at Safeway. There is always construction happening, no matter the hour, no matter the day. For us, there is something about leaving the country and heading down to Thailand that removes the grit and grime from our weary bodies. Thailand is the most laid back country I have ever been to. Everyone answers "yes" to everything, even if the answer should be "no." People are very casual about work and even their genders. I have had to do more explaining to my kids about why that man is wearing make-up and a mini skirt than I ever would have imagined.

Lots of people relocate to Thailand during retirement. Granted, most of the immigrants consist of older men looking for a younger Thai girlfriend. We even had a run in with an older British man that was petitioning to lower the age of the statutory rape laws in England. Lovely. Despite the Sodom-and-Gomorrah-like tendencies, it's a very easy place for foreigners to travel around. Now that we have been there several times, we have our favorites. Our favorite place for a greasy hamburger; a foot massage where little guppy fish bite off the extra skin from your feet; and the fried dough dripping in chocolate syrup and sweetened condensed milk. You can ride elephants and then watch them paint a picture with their trunks, walk around a monkey park, or raft on bamboo down the river.

One of our favorites is the Chiang Mai zoo. Normally, I hate zoos. As in, "I've cried at multiple zoos all around the world." I look into those poor gorillas' eyes and it's as if they are speaking to me like I'm Jane Goodall. They are telling me, "If someone doesn't get me out of this glass cage quickly, I'm gonna take this fake tree limb and pummel somebody." Chinese zoos are particularly disheartening. We've seen piglets jumping through hoops of fire, deer prancing around in concrete boxes, depressed St. Bernards chained in a steel cage, a 1,000 pound diabetic pig, and rabbits trying to burrow through a wooden cave. All of this has strengthened my resolve to be anti-zoo. But the zoo in Chiang Mai, is different. Minus the sweating penguins, all the animals are roaming about freely in a habitat similar to the one they came from. You can feed giraffes, rhinos, monkeys, and gazelles because only a three-foot fence separates them from you. While this does pose some safety issues, it makes for a fabulous zoo experience.

Whenever we are there we are also reminded of what it looks like to live in a place gripped by Buddhism. There are statues and altars to various gods everywhere. In the malls, on the playgrounds, outside the Starbucks, all of these places have their gods lined up to make sure spiritual appeasement is happening. Before you can start building, you will need to build a spirit house. The Thai believe that there is a guardian spirit for every piece of land, so when you build a house or business on it, you are taking away its home. In order to keep that spirit happy, you need to build it a home and give it satisfactory offerings to keep your family safe. As you ride around in a sung tow, you will often share a ride with monks who are scourging around local markets to pick up their morning alms from vendors. To earn merit from the monks, people will put out food and daily necessities in large baskets for the monks to pick up and use for the day.

While we always enjoy our time in Thailand, putting the wool blanket back on reminds us of our calling. It brings us comfort, even if the weight is heavy and cumbersome.

## shaming in the media

During the Olympics we saw a country try to wrap its mind around being hosts to the world. To a country ultimately concerned with security and censorship, the idea of opening themselves up like that is like ripping off a bandage from a wound not yet healed. They assume that opening up that bandage will only bring infection and corruption. In order to prevent those things, they feel they have to tighten the bandage and keep the wound from any outside elements.

About six months out from the 2008 Beijing Olympics, the government started circulating "good manners brochures." The people were told to start changing some life habits so as to make China a comfortable place for all the foreigners that would be descending upon them like the plague during the Olympic season. A few of these things included: not smoking in taxis, not shooting snot rockets from your nose, throwing your trash in a can instead of the street, and not peeing on public curbsides. The people were told that if they were caught smoking in a taxi, they would consequently be shamed in the media. This could include, but was not limited to, putting their face on the shaming channel on TV or slapping their mugshot on the shaming website. When I asked my friends about all of this, I got reactions of complete mortification. They could not fathom their faces being posted on any of these shaming sites. Some actually told us they would rather die. They could not bare the thought of making their families lose so much face.

As a rebellious American, I realized that my sense of shame is a little different. For most young Americans, having their mugshot shown on a website for defying the orders of smoking in a taxi would provoke a Tweet, a Facebook comment, and a blog post about the whole deal. They would provide the web address, time and date that their pictures would be posted, and a complete recounting of the shake down. They would be beaming with pride and this story would be told over and over again at beer-drenched Super bowl parties. These types of shaming sites might actually cause a rise in petty crime in the States.

A few years ago, we had a little visa mishap. One of our children's visas had expired. We had been in the process of working it out with the university where we had been studying Chinese, but it just didn't get wrapped up in time. When we went to renew our visas, we were met by a very stoic police officer. With a look of much consternation and maybe even a little delight, he told us that our visa had indeed expired. He told us we needed to pay a fine and that Jackson would be forced to write a self-deprecating letter of apology. This letter would act as a proverbial slap on the wrist for not getting this done on time. The letter was meant to teach us a lesson. In the letter, Jackson wrote that he was a horrible person and that only a tragic act of God, like a tsunami, could keep him from renewing his visa on time the next go around. The letter was dripping with hyperbole.

He went in the next week to turn in this letter of apology, giving it to the same Herculean police officer. Police guy read it, struck a crooked grin, and responded with much delight at the obvious face the foreigner must have lost at being forced to write such an embarrassing letter. We still have that letter. It's stored in our "funny things" folder on our hard drive.

Our police friend finally folded up the letter, put it in some file, and pasted our new visas into our passports. He ended up waiving the fine and then invited us over to his home to make dumplings.

### free stuff obsession

As with most of humanity, the Chinese love a good deal. If that deal also includes a free product, they will buy-in quickly. Most of the receipts at larger grocery stores have a scratch off section on the bottom half of the paper. While walking out of the store, you will see a black piece of sand paper and a sign on several walls. While passing by, people casually rub their receipts on this board to see if they have won. Those lucky ones who win a prize zip around the corner to pick up their bar of soap or bottle of juice. The prizes are very minimal, but it doesn't matter because for just that one instant, they have beat the system. They have overcome.

Throughout most stores, you will also notice free products taped to the item you are actually buying. Adhered to your 2 liter of Coke will be a washcloth; with your bag of chips will come a plastic bowl; a bowl of noodles will come with a free packet of pickled cabbage. All of them taped. All of them free. My personal favorite was a block of butter that had a free computer mouse taped securely to its side. I have now found myself bypassing the products without the free gifts and smiling proudly as I proceed to the check out with my box of cookies and free toothpick holder.

*gone again*

Jackson is traveling to the States to study for the next month. It is normal for him to leave for a week or two at a time, but usually it's in country and I know that if something major happened he could be here in a day or two. This time, I'm flying solo. The week before, I began to feel like a seventh grader walking into the lunchroom on the first day of school. Fears, doubts, despair and more fear crawled slowly into my thinking. My inner monologue went something like this: (my inner monologue is always in British English. I don't know why, it just is. Maybe it's my desire to feel like a sophisticated international spy) "What if one of my kids gets a broken arm while he's gone? What if they are paralyzed and then the rest of them come down with Tuberculosis, Leukemia, AIDS, and dysentery all in the same week?! There is NO way he can get back to help me take the life flight needed to get me to an international hospital!" These dramatic lines reel over and over in my head and slowly, my heart rate quickens and I start making sure I can locate passports, American cash, and a change of underwear in case we have to make a quick getaway. When you are swimming in fear, you flail around in uncertainty for so long that you tire quickly and eventually end up drowning in anger, impatience, and self-sufficiency.

You know when you are walking in a single file line and someone stops suddenly? Everyone else piles hard into the person who decided to stop stepping forward. The jolt gets sequentially harder and harder because of the compounding effect of people plowing into the back of you. On Friday, I stopped. The consequences have been felt ever since. I didn't purposefully stop, I just stopped thinking this Jackson-being-gone stuff was fun.

Oftentimes when he is gone, I give into my not-so-spiritual gifts. I find myself allowing little frustrations mushroom into complete anger. I let an inconvenience roll quickly into an impatient outrage. And honestly, I feel justified in all of these over the top reactions because I'm tired and life is hard. I use his being gone as a reason to make compost out of the fruit of the spirit that the Lord has given me (Gal. 5:22). See, when I became an adopted child of God's, he gave me love, joy, peace, patience, kindness, goodness, faithfulness, gentleness, and self-control. As His child, I already possess those things. So when I choose to not demonstrate self-control or patience, it is sin. I am choosing to not display something the Lord has already given to me. I have found over and over again that when life is hard and dumps more in our cup than we can handle, whatever spills over is whatever was in the cup to begin with. If my cup is already filled with impatience, frustration, and doubt, then when life is squeezing me in, those things will pour out.

I want this time to be different. I want to be so enthralled with Jesus that there is no room in my mind for selfish musings about the fears of being alone with five kids, thousands of miles from my husband. I want to wake up trusting the hand of the Lord for my day. I want to silence the voices that tell me that I'm not strong enough or patient enough to do this for a month. Those same voices that whisper fears to me early in the morning. Those same voices that told the Israelites that living in captivity was better than trusting in the provisions of the Lord. Instead of giving those voices room to speak, I want to allow for the "God of all comfort" (2 Cor. 1:3) to raise my head in confidence and joy.

## Chinese workforce

Every once in a while, we get passionate people who email to tell us that they are praying for the wall of Communism to crumble here. While I understand the cultural momentum wrapped up in this prayer request, I never know quite what to say. You see, for most Americans, Communism is equated with Nazi Germany. So in their minds, China is an oppressive, dangerous place. They imagine streets lined with armed police and legions of armies chanting cadences as we make our morning oatmeal. This is just not the case. We stay far away from politics here, but I will say that the one thing the government does provide for its people is jobs. The jobs might be meager, but people are employed. We have seen young women wrapping oranges in plastic bags; women using tree branches tied together to sweep the streets; young men in charge of the yogurt aisle at the grocery store. All of these jobs are helping people keep food in their mouths and at least some scant shelter over their family's heads. These things might seem slow and maybe even useless, but all of them are jobs.

When you walk into a grocery store, each employee is in charge of a five-foot by five-foot space. So if you happen to find yourself with a need for salt, you should to ask the salt attendant. If you are standing in the rice aisle and you ask for salt, you will get a shy, "I don't know." Now, instead of getting frustrated, I wander around until I find my salt lady. And when you find that salt lady, she will hover over you and try to help until you buy something. While we were in the States, I found myself wandering aimlessly trying to find a salt lady or a bacon man. None were to be found. Eight months later and there were still things that I couldn't find because nobody hovered the aisles. I have grown to appreciate the overstaffed grocery stores that we use here.

When we first moved to China, my industrious mind walked around making things more efficient. If they would just hire a street sweeping machine instead of tying together dead tree branches to use as brooms, things would not only be cleaner, but faster; don't worry about wrapping fruit that God already gave a peel, like a banana or an orange; buy a tall ladder instead of stringing together rods of bamboo. As I envisioned all of these efficiencies, I also stared into the faces of the people who would be jobless had efficiency been the goal. The fleet of five street sweepers would be reduced to one street sweeping truck driver. The five ladies wrapping oranges would be told to go home. The girl managing the yogurt aisle would have to find another place to stand. We Americans value efficiency and purpose. There is really very little purpose in wrapping an orange in plastic. My first inclination was to get rid of the excess. But, in this case, the excess had a child to feed and a wife to provide for. When I shift my eyes to the stories behind the inefficiency, all of the sudden it doesn't look so trivial. It looks more like a concerned father tending to the needs of his children.

## *rarely early, but always on time*

Four of our children will be having Children's Day festivities at their school tomorrow morning. The parents are expected to come and they should prepare snacks. When did we find out about this little affair? This afternoon when I picked them up. The fact that we even knew about this a solid 13 hours before needing to be there is a vast improvement. When my husband taught English at a local university, he would be waiting Sunday night for a phone call that told him what classes he would be teaching that Monday morning. The phone would ring and the Dean of the English department would enthusiastically tell Jackson that he would be teaching British literature and linguistics. Just because we speak English doesn't mean we know much about British literature. So we would scramble for the BBC rendition of anything Jane Austen. We don't learn the phonetic alphabet in America, so linguistics can be a bit daunting. And with both of us having grown up in Texas, there is no guarantee that we actually did conquer 8th grade grammar.

We would then plan a few icebreakers to get him through the first class so that lesson planning could begin Monday night. We have tried asking for the schedule a few weeks ahead and we receive looks like we just asked them if they wear boxers or briefs. They don't understand why we need to know our teaching schedule three weeks in advance. The Dean of the English Department will simply tell us when we need to know. We would often get phone calls at 2:00 in the afternoon inviting us to a large banquet in our honor. It would start at 5:00…that night. We would throw ourselves through the shower (because certainly it had been at least five days since we'd last seen the inside of our shower curtain) and rush to seat ourselves before the toasting and speeches began.

I've tried booking airplane tickets a month in advance. No go. I've tried making doctor appointments at large Western hospitals in large modern cities. Nope. Need a hotel room for your parents who flew 27 hours to come and visit? Just come in that morning and we will get you one.

I am a planner and this has driven me crazy on more than one occasion. But I'm learning. You see, I'm addicted to information. Many times I just want to know and be on the "inside." I won't actually be able to do anything with the information, I just want it. I've realized how often I do this with the Lord. I have discovered the hard way that the Lord actually works more often like our Dean of the English Department friend. The Lord gets much delight in revealing His plans to His children, but it's the timing of His telling us that can make us antsy, impatient kids. When I look back at times the Lord has told our family what decision to make, I've found that He is very rarely early in telling us, but He is never, ever too late. So apparently if He hasn't told me where to go or what to do yet, I don't need to know. And I'd probably screw something up if I had the information anyway. God knows that about me. He knows that about all of us.

We have seen the Lord rescue us at the last minute many times. Two years ago, we started the adoption process. Once we decided to adopt, we threw all our weight into the process.

After the stock market plummeted, we realized that the process was going to stretch us both spiritually and financially. The Lord prodded several families to help out, they gave generously to help us bring Joi home. Even after that, we had about half of the amount that we would need to finish the process. We called my parents, who also help take care of our finances stateside, and told them we wanted to liquidate all our savings. We were confident that Joi was already a member of our family, so we needed to do whatever it took to get her home.

When you are sure of the Lord's will, there is little pain in a sacrifice. Whenever people ask us about how the finances worked out, I remind them that when God is in something, He'll get it done. Sometimes He will get it done through longer hours at the office, other times he will do it through the generosity of others. In our case, He finished off the process through the US government. Still needing about half of the cost of our adoption, we siphoned off a majority of our savings. It was at this point that my husband decided it was time to start a PhD program. This made sense to us because, again, the Lord never asks us to do things that we can actually accomplish on our own. Not sure how we would pay for all of this, he applied and we prayed. I want to be careful here to not promote health and wealth gospel junk. The pastors propagating health and wealth make me angry. As in, if I saw them in the store, I would want to kick them in the shins and flip their grocery carts. We have had the Lord provide for us through giving us 4 jobs and lots of pain. And there have been times where He has dropped checks in the mail, but all of these are His provisions. In this particular season of our family's life, God decided to drop a big fat money bomb into our world.

The week after Jackson decided to start his PhD program, Obama's health care plan got approved. Tucked neatly into part of the 85 million-page document was a provision for families that were adopting. Each family that finalized their adoptions in 2011 would receive a substantial check as a refund from the government. Simply save a receipt from your adoption agency, and the IRS would refund a five-figure amount to us at tax time.

We didn't expect that when we started out in the adoption process. We certainly didn't expect the US government to foot half of the bill to bring our daughter home, but God knew all along how He was planning on getting Joi home. Rarely early, but always on time.

# Rescuing the Holidays

Once again we find ourselves enmeshed in the
Holiday Season, that very special time of year when we join
with our loved ones in sharing centuries-old traditions such
as trying to find a parking space at the mall. We traditionally
do this in my family by driving around the parking lot until
we see a shopper emerge from the mall, then we follow her, in
very much the same spirit as the Three Wise Men, who 2,000
years ago followed a star, week after week, until it
led them to a parking space.

Dave Berry

*Being pulled from the pile-up of American holidays, we have been given a chance to reflect of what they all actually mean. The depth of a holiday tradition should not be measured in how much we conform, but how well our hearts celebrated its true meaning.*

### giving your ancestors an ipad

Every springtime here brings the Sweeping of the Tombs Festival. Some city dwellers will return to their villages to spend time with family and sacrifice to their ancestors. Others will take the allotted two days off of work to head out to Shanghai or Beijing and spend their money on lovely touristy type things.

This year was interesting because we have moved further down South where they are much more outwardly religious than the Northeast. I am rubbing shoulders with monks on the buses and gazing at temples as I drop the kids off at school in the morning. Each family member is to purchase a paper replica of something that they think their ancestors could use in the afterlife. Then they take these objects and burn them in a small bonfire on the side of a street or next to their loved one's gravesite. The most common things that people buy are paper copies of money, cars, new clothes or cell phones. Most of these things can be bought on the street or in any store. As you pass through the produce section, you can pick up your sacrifices to be offered after dinner.

But this year, Steve Jobs made a splash in the shallow ancestor worship pond. People were stocking up on the iPad 2 and iPhone 4 paper replicas. These are the latest and greatest generation of Apple products. The replicas came with a picture of the start-up screen and were selling out the second they hit the streets. Although some people were concerned that their deceased great grandparents wouldn't be able to operate such a modern gadget and so stuck with burning money instead. Others were disappointed that the newest generation was sold out and so settled with buying the first generation iPad. It would no doubt be offered with a sense of sorrow at the substandard offering.

When Sweeping of the Tombs comes around, my heart always sinks. The smoke from their sacrifices is making their ability to accept truth a murky pursuit. As the fires engulf the sacrifices, the people feel that the penance has been paid to satisfy the longings of people who are rotting in a grave.

Sweeping of the Tombs is an outward expression of an inward captivity. You walk through the ashes that were burned in hopeful ransom and duty the night before. It makes my soul ache. When you stare at the ashes being drawn up by the wind, it looks as if they are chasing something. But what are they chasing? Nothing. They are actually being forced by the wind into activity. Ashes only do what ashes can do which is to follow the wind. The hearts of the Chinese are doing what they have always done or seen done in their culture. They aren't questioning or asking why burning an iPad is so important to their springtime festival. They just do it because they are told that sacrifice to ancestors is an essence of being Chinese.

As I walk through the swirling ashes, I pray. I try to allow the pursuits of vanity in my own life be drawn out and sacrificed to the Lord. Where do I fall in line culturally, allowing my affections to be choked out by vanity?

A few months ago, when grappling with this very thing as we celebrated Thanksgiving and Christmas in America, I wrote about waking up as believers-about not allowing ourselves to be lulled asleep to dream about fitting in and keeping up.

### stupid things we do to celebrate

I really do love celebrations, but sometimes we just glide through so many of them, completely missing any implications for our souls. When I was driving around in the early fall, I was still in shock at how big Halloween had grown in the States. I'm just gonna say it: Halloween is the dumbest holiday on the calendar. Christopher Columbus Day ranks up there pretty close, especially considering history is not on his side. I passed a Presbyterian church with ghosts, pumpkins, and hairy spiders in their webs. A church. Exalting Halloween. I passed Christians saying to one another, "Happy Halloween" and asking their children which animated character they want to be on the 31ˢᵗ.

People say, "Well, we don't do the scary stuff. We keep it light." But aren't we still celebrating the idea of Halloween?

Then we head to Thanksgiving and we celebrate "family." For many, family becomes an idol during Thanksgiving and we accept it by using the word thankful to describe our misplaced worship of family. We say that this is the holiday for families to come visit and share life together. We get together, eat till we're sick and watch the Cowboys lose again. I'm not sure the Pilgrims did any of that. Except watch the Cowboys lose. They've been doing that for awhile now.

The pilgrims were desperately thankful to the Lord of Lords for saving them from starvation. For providing a place to worship in freedom. But very rarely do we honor the Lord for His provisions to us during a Thanksgiving meal. I often forget that there is even a spiritual meaning behind the holiday.

Then Christmas. Don't even get me started on Christmas. I have been known to rant and rave about the fat guy in his little red coat. We won't do Santa, and this year we're not doing presents. And you know what, most of the people that give us a hard time about this are professing Christians. They say that we are denying our kids some magical moment. As if the Polar Express is supposed to careen through our hearts and help us believe in this mysterious thing called the "Christmas Spirit." In my opinion, the whole thing is ridiculous, really. There's this undefined pressure that tells us to find peace and harmony. These are all phrases the world is using to define the exhaustion we feel as fallen human beings hunting for things to rescue us.

Buying presents isn't sinful. Getting together with family isn't a sin. But diminishing the Savior for anything else is.

I don't admit to having arrived in this Christian walk, but as believers, we are to question the cultural norms. Why do we celebrate the things we do in American culture? Should I also celebrate them? Do they butt up against any of my beliefs as a Christ follower?

Too often, we just accept the cultural norms as the standards for our family. We are far from perfect parents, but one thing we can give to our kids is a mind that thinks through these types of things. To not just blindly pummel through holiday after holiday without examining what that means for us as believers. Sometimes I think we forget that as Christians, we are weird. We will stick out. We will make decisions that our friends and family might not understand. But if we are seeking Scripture and communicating these things in grace, then God is pleased.

I see too many parents concerned that their kids fit in and are popular. You know what, if they are striving to live like Christ, they aren't going to fit in. Jesus made decisions that were constantly pulling him apart from the culture at hand. And I'm not too sure that being popular should be the ultimate standard that we hold up for our children anyway. Jesus was pretty unpopular and most of His friends fled while He was left for criminal execution on a cross.

We need to step back and examine why we do things as believers. We need to be intentional about what and how we celebrate. We have to make sure that striving to be like Christ supersedes our desires to be liked and needed.

I know this categorizes me in the obnoxious, boycott Disney, wear turtlenecks and don't let your girls get their ears pierced category, but I'm tired of Christians sitting on the sidelines, accepting culture as the norm in all these areas. We are quickly becoming a fainting, flickering light, destined to be extinguished.

### santa fiasco

As a disclaimer: you've been warned that I have issues with Santa and the way Christmas is celebrated in the States. Clear your mind, light a hazelnut candle and grab a chai tea. These things will help you not want to throw your book across the room and write me hateful emails at two in the morning. After this, I won't mention Santa again. Promise.

The Christmas season has come and gone and it went better than planned, but not without a lot of effort on our part. The wealth was overwhelming for us. The exorbitance was too much. At the stores, people ran around frantically shoving toys into their baskets as if to fill them up with obligation and guilt. I've never seen people so frustrated, tired, and joyless.

After living overseas for several years, we vowed to never be in the States for Christmas. I would rather amputate my big toe with dental floss than spend a Christmas in the States. When we found out that Joi's blood ordeal was going to keep us here through Christmas, I had to take a deep breath. I was going to be faced with the tangle of consumerism that has trapped Christmas, wrapped it up in its web and sucked it dry. A better part of me wanted to go shopping for non-perishables and just hunker down in the house for the entire month of December. But then when I realized that Christmas displays creep their way out in September, I surrendered to dealing with it head on. Besides, staying inside with very little human contact for a month made me feel like a crazy mom from Montana who wanted to nurse her children until they were eight.

The amount of preparation that goes into making sure each person has some magical memory is mind blowing. Families turn their cheeks to years of conflict to sit at dinner together and pretend like Dec. 26th might never come. As if they can stay in a perpetual state of being whimsically unaware of the relational chasm that gets bigger year after year. People try and fill that mountainous gap with shiny new toys and a peaceful dinner at home.

We decided as a family to let the kids research charities to give their money to. We picked four different ones and gave money to each. It was fantastic to listen to my 7 year old son talk about supporting workers in the Middle East, to hear my daughter get excited about purchasing goats for Ethiopian farmers. It brought my Christmas morning more joy to see them excited to give to others than it would have been to watch them open tons of gifts. Some Christians justify the celebration of Santa by pulling the St. Nick card and celebrating the historical

Santa. But, as far as I understand, the historical St. Nick went around giving gifts away to those in need, not spoiling his nieces with Hannah Montana nail appliqués. So if you want to go the St. Nick route, that still puts a wedge in the plans to spoil kids.

Every Christmas, many Christians ponder (or at least should ponder) whether to tell their kids the truth about Santa.

First, Jesus gets less honor when kids' (and our) attention is given more to a make believe fat guy who will give gifts according to our good deeds, not grace.

The fact that people don't see the harm in Santa illustrates how easy it is to not treasure the name of Christ-to forget that He should be supreme in the human heart and therefore be most valued during Christmas. It's a heart issue: what are we most excited, talking and thinking about? Our kids? What are they most excited, talking and thinking about during Christmas? Is the amount of exposure to Christ outweighing the time spent pondering all things Santa?

Second, it hurts our kids. How? First, it deprives them of the annual chance to single-mindedly think on the gospel, the good news of Christ's coming. Do we think so little of it that we would allow for distractions? The greatest way to love anyone, kids included, is to help them savor the glory of Christ. It would be absurd for us to celebrate Dora the Explorer or Mickey Mouse more than my son on his birthday. Then why do we do that for Jesus and His birth?

Third, besides our kids, other people who watch our lives miss out on seeing that Jesus matters as much as He does! This is one of the easiest and most clear ways Christians can stick out-as they should.

Fourth, for many kids, it sends confusing signals about trust when they find out that their parents and teachers have lied to them. Someone very close to me has this testimony of hurt because they felt deceived and foolish by believing in Santa as a child.

In short, people perpetuate the Santa story because they want their kids to have an experience or a feeling this time of year. A feeling or experience isn't the problem. The issue is that people don't think Jesus is satisfying enough and is in fact the source of better "experiences" and "feelings."

I wish that Christian families would pull back and not assume that all things cultural are things to embrace.

## dragon boat festival

Dragon Boat Festival is celebrated every June in China. The government allows schools and businesses to take Monday off to celebrate and relax with family. While the actual celebrations are more festive and fun, the tradition behind this holiday is rather grim. There are several ideas as to the legends behind this holiday, but the most popular is that of China's first known poet named Qu Yuan. He was a statesman and deeply loved his country. At that time, there were warring states and consolidation of powers. He had advised the King of Chu not to sign a peace treaty, but the suspicious King did it anyway. The King of Chu thought that Qu Yuan was simply trying to make a name for himself. When Chu eventually got overthrown by a larger state, Qu decided the loss was too much. On the 5th day of the 5th month on the lunar calendar, he held onto a large boulder, jumped into the Miluo River, and drowned. Each year, the Dragon Boat Festival is supposed to honor him. For others, the festival involves paying homage to the god of water so that he will bless the year's crops.

In light of this, when our friend, Tom, walked in yesterday morning, I asked how he and his family celebrated. Both he and his sweet wife are strong Christians and long to look different as Chinese followers of Christ. His response was, "We don't celebrate Dragon Boat Festival because it glorifies ghosts." I would say that for most people here, the holiday represents a time to gather with friends and have a good meal, but for Tom, he believed that by engaging in this celebration, he would be compromising his testimony. I wouldn't say that all believers feel this same conviction, but it was interesting to hear him and his stance on things. This is a hard thing for the believers here because there is no space for non-conformity. To not go along with these traditions and festivals is to deny being Chinese. We have heard over and over again that we Americans celebrate Christmas and the Chinese celebrate Chinese New Year. Our brothers and sisters here incur much isolation when these holidays roll around. And each time, they have to decide where to throw their allegiance.

The Chinese are also very superstitious. They'll spend a lot more money to get a telephone number that has no 4's in it because the number 4 and the word for death are very similar, so they think that it will bring bad luck and an early death. Couples refuse to have babies in the zodiac year of the Tiger because those children will be stubborn and unruly. People will refuse to sweep their homes on the day of Chinese New Year for fear of removing the fortune from the family. While these things can be classified as cultural intrigues, for many it is truly a gripping belief system that deafens their ears from hearing the truth.

# Your Day Tomorrow

"But I do not account my life of any value nor as precious to myself, if only I may finish my course and the ministry that I received from the Lord Jesus."

Acts 20:24 (ESV)

*Since we know the Great Commission commands believers to be a part of reaching the nations, why not make that your default calling from the Lord? Why should we assume that the Lord is calling people to stay in America unless He says otherwise? I say that more people should assume they are called to go unless the Lord tells them to stay in America.*

### packing a bag

This section is sort of a soapbox parenthesis. Living overseas has become a bit of a fad these last few years, as if we walk down the streets in China alongside dancing dragons, airy flutes playing in the background, while sipping jasmine tea with monks all day long. There are things our family gets to do and see because we live here and I wouldn't trade them for anything. We are blown away that the Lord would allow such oafs to do what we get to do on a daily basis, but it's also hard. Days are long. Frustrations are many. I don't want to discourage people from moving out of the States to follow a calling or dream, but there needs to be preparation if you are going to flourish.

Following Christ should encompass your entire being. Living in another culture simply complicates things a bit. Whether our neighbor eats with chopsticks or grills steaks, we are called to love and serve those around us. Working as an English teacher, home schooling your children, or running a Fortune 500 company each make you define your "home" in terms of your identity in Christ. If you are looking to serve overseas, I think there are a few things to think through.

1.  Show Him as big. Big enough that the culture shock and struggles will seem like child's play on days that are disastrously hard. You make Him big by pursuing Scripture-the black and white truths of Scripture that sometimes can butt up against the "truths" you learned as a child. But be patient and allow your view of God to widen and your view of self to shrink.

2.    Start sharing Christ with anyone and everyone. You see, if you wait for your heart to "be broken for the lost" or to feel "compassion for the lost," you will end up not sharing and feeling defeated. To try and conjure emotions for a stranger is hard and usually not realistic. Share Jesus because He is good news.

3.    Read anything by John Piper, especially *Let the Nations Be Glad*. Also pick up Bob Sjogren's *Unveiled at Last*, and David Platt's *Radical*. All of these will challenge you shift your paradigms and set you into action.

4.    Ask questions that may seem simple, but at a deep heart level can be extremely hard to answer. For example, are you going to believe Jesus? Not in the walk down the aisle type of way. But in the way that you will believe him even when he says things that drive thousands of people away. Including some of his best friends and followers. Do you honestly believe Romans 8:28 when it says that God can work out all things for the good of those who love him? Because living overseas isn't about checking off a box on an experience. It's not about patting ourselves on the back and sharing amazing pictures with friends.

   Reaching the world is about Jesus. It's not about you or your desire for an overseas experience. Secondly, are you going to obey and trust Jesus? Or will you listen and walk away and look the same today as you were yesterday. Will you continue to limp through life being drawn like a moth to a light on a warm summer's evening? What are the consequences of living a life that truly believes and trusts all of Jesus' words? All of Jesus' words.

5.    Pray over your relationships. Maybe you are in a relationship right now and you are scared to answer a calling to go overseas. Or you are wondering what a move will do to a relationship. Maybe it means you will be

single for several years. The bottom line is that if you are overwhelmed with what moving overseas will do to your relationships, you are consumed with the wrong thing.

When you are so wholly satisfied in Christ, the working-out of a particular relationship becomes secondary. It doesn't mean it's not hard or that you aren't going to have to make some difficult decisions. But I want to say that instead of spending sleepless nights thinking about how things will work out, drown your desires in worship and Scripture. Pray over what to do with that relationship, but spend an even longer time worshipping Jesus. Turn your head towards Him. If you KNOW that Jesus wants you to live overseas and your boyfriend is adamant that he will live in the US, then you need to re-evaluate. For others, this might mean leaving a strong church community to move out to a poor village. These can be scary life transitions.

I've had so many friends cast away their callings to live overseas because they put their relationships in a place of idolatry. And they justified away their call so that they could remain in that relationship. If you are married, then be patient. God is not going to call one spouse and not the other. So, if one of you wants to move overseas tomorrow and the other is looking to set up home in the States, then submit yourselves in prayer together as a couple. He is calling you to the same thing because you are now one. This is going to require patience and perseverance for both of you.

6. Learn to be flexible and to suffer. A Chinese friend of ours was really upset one day. When asked what was wrong, he replied, "I'm ready to suffer for my faith! All my friends have been questioned by officials, and I'm ready to bear witness too!" How are you living NOW that is training you to count the cost? Are you going to dark, dingy places and ministering among the outcasts of society? Are you going to uncomfortable corners in conversations with friends and

family members? Are you finding international students on college campuses or inviting that colleague over for dinner to love and minister and share Jesus with?

Chances are, not every single person reading this is going to live overseas. Some of you will be mothers with children crawling at your feet and others will go on to own a small business, but your call to be concerned with global lostness is the same. You are also called to bring the gospel to the nations, discipling and baptizing. We often tell people that you are either called to go or send or you are being disobedient. What will that look like for you? What is that one thing that is keeping you from accepting a call from the Lord to work overseas? How are you contending for the church worldwide as you live here in the States?

When you move overseas, things will go wrong... weekly. Apart from loving Jesus, I tell people that you need to be flexible. Don't expect to find the familiar because you are no longer in North America, and to expect anything less than that is naive. Use this new culture to stretch your definition of 'normal' and try to learn why the people are doing what they are doing. Usually there is a method to the madness and instead of just shoving an experience into a negative category, make an effort to understand the reasoning behind it. You just might expose some of your assumptions along the way that need to be adjusted and tweaked.

7. Be Uncomfortable. "Foxes have holes and birds of the air have nests, but the Son of Man has no place to lay his head." Jesus didn't even have the comfort of knowing he had a bed to rest on. We are called to a place of inconvenience and discomfort. Put yourselves there. Go home and find a way to make yourself uncomfortable for the name of Jesus and the sake of preparing yourself to live overseas. Get rid of cable or trade in your iPhone for a cheap one. Start eating a more meager diet so as to adjust your body's expectations of daily need.

But we have to be careful not to turn into legalistic Pharisees. Jesus desires worship and not sacrifice. You simply are looking for ways to make yourself less and Jesus more. You are looking for ways to train your mind, body, and soul to flourish overseas.

8. Be involved. Finally, pray over being involved in the reaching of unreached people groups. God promises that every tongue, tribe, and nation will bow before him and call him Lord. If that is going to happen in our lifetime, people will need to join God in reaching the more than 6,000 unreached people groups in this world. Unreached People Groups (UPGs) are those distinct groups with less than 2% of the population existing as evangelical Christians and less than 5% Christian of any kind. Cults are popping up like crazy in places around Asia. The church is young and in desperate need of training.

As you find yourself in high school, college, or the working world…pray. Pray for your brothers and sisters around the world. Pray for the lost; for the gospel to go forth. Prayer is not an asterisk to reaching the nations. It is the arm by which the Lord extends Himself to the desperate and hurting. As you think about moving overseas, submit yourself to being there long term. So many people coincidently get "called" back to America after about two years overseas. I find it intriguing that it's also about that time that things get hard. No longer is the kid running around peeing on the sidewalk funny. No longer is listening to drunk businessmen sing John Denver at 2:00 in the morning a fun cultural moment. After two years, you have a new home. But just as I would never imagine leaving a two-year-old child to fend for himself, I need to stay where God has put me. To leave early is to leave a child and abandon a people. Not everyone is called to live their lives in another country, but I am asserting that it just might be more than one might expect.

Living overseas isn't for the noble or the brave. It isn't some life you pursue because you think it would be charming to tell people at a dinner party that you just flew in from Hong Kong. Sometimes it feels like living overseas is reserved for the ill equipped and foolish. It is a calling given to people who don't mind being called an idiot for taking their children 8,000 miles away. It is for those people who have found God giving them secure moments of grace while the world is shouting promises of money and comfort.

To make it overseas, you've got to come to the end of yourself.

C.S. Lewis said, "Miracles are a retelling in small letters of the very same story which is written across the whole world in letters too large for some of us to see."

Don't miss the small letters.
Don't allow the words of parents or friends convince you that a life overseas is wasted.
Don't be lulled to sleep with the comforts found in the States.

Pursue the uncomfortable.
Pursue the gospel.
Pursue grace because grace has already pursued you.

Each of these moments of clarity is treasured because it allows us to see clearly what is ahead and in turn reminds us that what we have seen is from God.

# Acknowledgments

This list of acknowledgments could extend for several pages. My brain is entirely too disorganized to have completed this task alone. My supportive husband told me that if I was committed to finishing this task (something I'm notoriously horrible at) then he was fully behind it. He has truly been a foundation of encouragement and rational thinking for me. My editing friends Stephanie, Becky, Ortons, Kristen, Amanda, Kellie, Masseys, Regina, DY, Brad, Bensons, Lexi, Laura, Altics, St. Michels, and both of my parents. Travis, you put up with my addiction to commas, misplaced tenses and book titles. Your patience and editing prowess was a huge help. Thank you for all of your insights. They are valued and treasured.

To the Howards and the Wells for your graphic support and artistic eye. My sister, Kim, for answering my phone calls and indulging my indecision. All of you are so gifted and did an incredible job with the art process. Everyone at Lucid Books, you guys are a great group to work with.

My kids. For showing me grace and laughter so clearly. You add color and texture to our days. Thank you for letting me pour out our lives so that others will hopefully be blessed.

To all my friends in China. For sharing your stories with me and allowing me to laugh, cry, scratch my chin and ask questions. Thank you for making me feel normal, even if it's just for 2 minutes.

Ten years ago, you told me to start writing. I told you no… lots. Donna, thank you for gently pushing and reminding me that God is bigger than any ability I could try and muster up.

And to so many for praying for our family as we stumble our way through each day. Your consistency and loyalty to Jesus is humbling. Our weekly prayer team. You guys blow me away as you faithfully contend on our behalf.

For all the pastors and musicians that kept me sane. Through technology, you whispered truth loud enough to drown out the lies I so frequently rehearse in my mind.

The community around the world that loves us and speaks into our lives blows my mind. I don't deserve the grace of friendship that we have found.

Without Jesus and His intervention in my heart, I would still be a wandering sinner in need of rescuing. I could not live over here just for the adventure of it. But knowing that "The Lord redeems the life of his servants; none of those who take refuge in him will be condemned" (Psalms 34:22) gives me hope that I am His. Forever.

# Story Index

## Who We Are

## American Culture Shock

## Moving in with Uncle Sam

## Transition and Moist: Two Words I Hate

## Letting the Dust Settle

## Squatty Potties and Other Realities

## Family Ties

## Life Over Here

## Rescuing the Holidays

## Your Day Tomorrow

CPSIA information can be obtained at www.ICGtesting.com
Printed in the USA
LVOW091408070312

272031LV00001B/12/P